AFRICA IN LATE 1960

THE RELUCTANT AFRICAN

THE RELUCTANT AFRICAN

BY LOUIS E. LOMAX

HARPER & BROTHERS, PUBLISHERS, NEW YORK

THE RELUCTANT AFRICAN

Printed in the United States of America

A-L

Library of Congress catalog card number: 60-16472

TO "MISS FANNIE"
She had faith when no one else did.

AFRICA IN LATE 1960

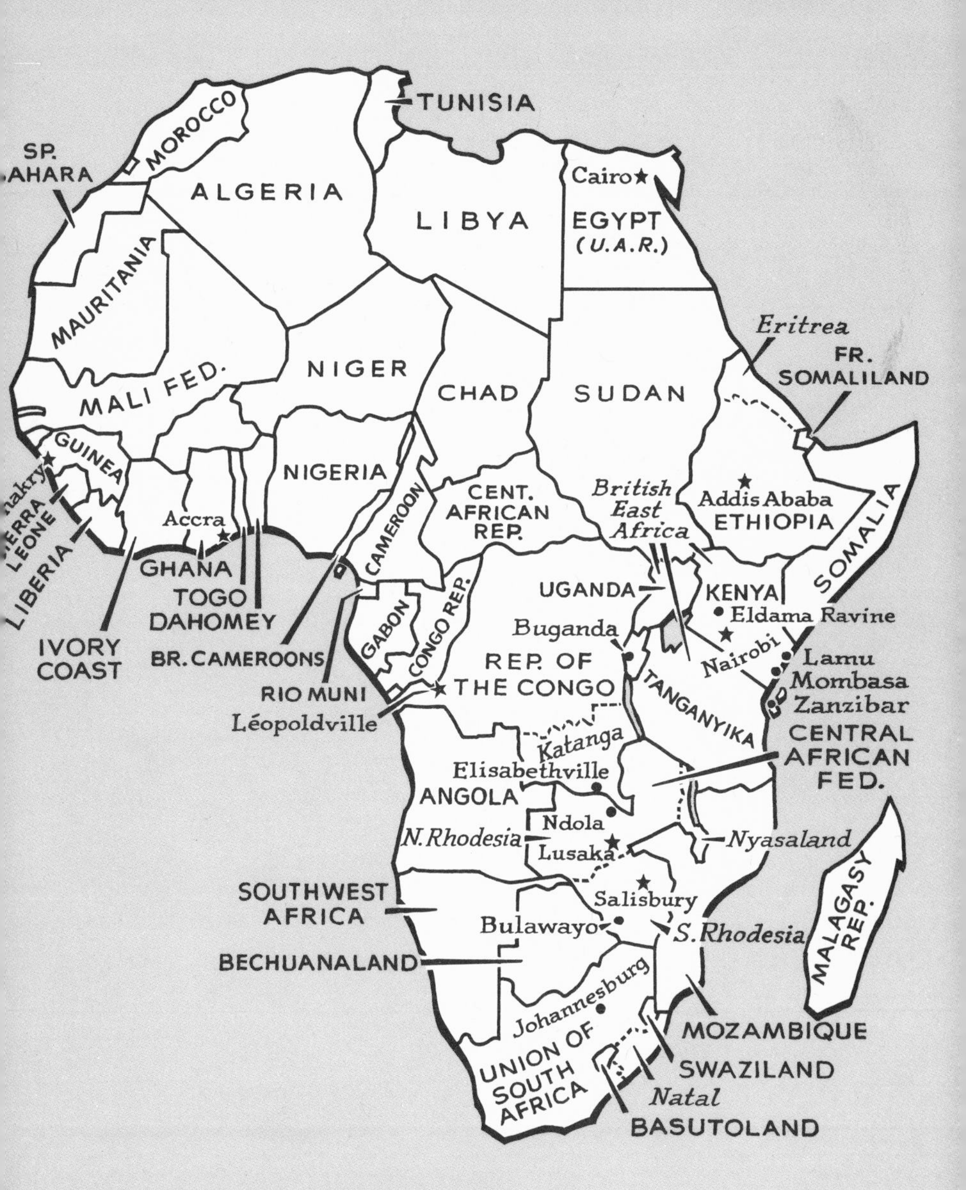

THE RELUCTANT AFRICAN

"No, no, no!" the man to my left shouted, almost choking on a swallow of beer. "Africans are not 'natives'!" At the word "natives" he banged his half-empty glass into the center of the square café table. "Never call Africans 'natives,'" he continued, shaking his finger didactically in my face. The much younger man sitting to my right smiled and nodded in agreement.

I was embarrassed, engulfed by a feeling of stupidity. I looked around to see if other patrons of the café had heard the outburst. No one had; if they had they did not show it. They were preoccupied with their table companions; to a man almost, they silently patted their feet to the music of the juke box. For a long, anxious moment I eyed the men on either side of me. I wondered if they were serious, for after all it had never occurred to me that an indigenous people were maligned or insulted if one called them "natives."

"I meant no harm. . . ."

"It is not what you meant," the man to my left interrupted. "It is what the Africans will *think* you mean if you call them 'natives.' They hate the word. It is a stigma of inferiority, a badge of inherent backwardness pinned on the Africans by the colonialists.

"Now get these things firmly rooted in your mind," he continued. "Africans are Africans . . . *not* natives! . . . *not* Negroes! And as far as the Africans are concerned, no white man is an African! They are *Europeans, Americans* or just plain *white men.* But *Africans?* Never! It doesn't matter a damn how long he or his ancestors have been in Africa, he is NOT an African."

"And another thing," the younger man interposed, correcting yet another of my innocent mistakes, "don't refer to African homes as 'huts.' They are homes, just like your split-level out in Queens.

"The trouble with most American Negroes," he added, "is that when they go to Africa they go just like the white man: they think like him; they act like him; they react as he reacts. That is why they don't get to see too much; that is why they don't understand what little they do see."

We three black men were seated at a table in the Red Rooster, the favorite haunt of Harlem's black bourgeoisie. The man to my left, a gifted American intellectual and former lecturer at New York University, had just returned from Africa, where for four years he had served as economic adviser to one of the independent states. The younger man was a student from Kenya now studying in the United States. In a week I would be off for a two months' reporter's tour of Africa south of the Sahara, to meet the men who are generating the wind of change Prime Minister Macmillan feels blowing through that entire continent; I would sit in on closed meetings, see African politicians at work in unguarded moments, go behind the emotional façade of freedom and be given a candid view of the economic, political and personal power forces now at work in Africa. My African contacts, here and in Africa, had warned me, however, that if I really wanted to understand what I saw and heard I must first be turned into an African. I must think black, feel black, act black, love black, demonstrably suspect everything and anything nonblack, and talk black—a new jargon peculiar to African nationalists; a patois designed to adulate everything black, to deprecate everything white. My two table companions had kindly offered to teach me the art of being an African. I had come to learn.

The three subsequent sessions, as well as that first one, were not easy for my tutors or for me. Their anguish, however, was fleeting, a momentary disgust with an argumentative student. Mine was deeper; I did not know it then, but my anguish was to linger.

"You are going to die from an overdose of integration yet," the former N.Y.U. lecturer told me when I suggested that multiracialism was the better part of common sense in a place like Kenya. The prediction was made lightly, in good humor. But I knew how true it could be. Like most American Negroes, I have an irrevocable commitment to integration. It is our new faith, our contribution to the moral and political evolution of man as a social being. Without integration we Negroes come unglued, democracy fails, morality cracks, nothing adds up. And as one who has helped shape that faith by reporting from Little Rock, Sturgis-Clay, Kentucky, Clinton, Tennessee, and from the banks of a burdened Mississippi River as it yielded up the battered and lynched body of Emmett Till, I cannot accept any form of racial separatism.

But we three men were not playing games! We were not plotting a stunt. Nor were we there to coddle my preconceived notions about the imperativeness of white and black men living together as one throughout the earth. We were there, rather, to condition me to feel and understand the anguish of a troubled people of an even more troubled land.

It was late in May, 1960. Serious trouble was brewing in Africa. The Congo was surging toward freedom; men who knew the raw facts of life in the Congo predicted there would be trouble—serious racial trouble—there. The Kikuyu tribesmen of Kenya were quietly and clandestinely reviving oath-taking; informed Africans sensed the threat of a new Mau Mau movement. There was unrest in the Rhodesias, and strange noises were coming from Ethiopia.

The recent killings at Sharpville, South Africa (brought on by African revolt against the pass laws), had galvanized black Africa's determination to unite and rid all Africa of colonialism and white domination.

"There can be no peace or security in Africa without political freedom," Ghana Prime Minister Kwame Nkrumah said just before I left New York. "As long as one inch of African soil remains under colonial rule there will be strife and conflict. . . . There will be insecurity for the oppressors and constant resentment and revolt on the part of the oppressed. These are the elementary facts of life in Africa today."

It was my job to examine the matrix of these elementary facts of African life; to live with the Africans south of the Sahara, find out how they think and why; to suffer their pains and walk with them in search of relief. It was a story, I regret to say, no white reporter could get in today's Africa. The Africans suspected me, too, for a while. ("You bear the credentials of the 'white press,'" one of them told me. "Even if you wrote the truth they would not print it.") But in time a mystical thing called the black brotherhood—understood,

I am certain, only by the Africans—engulfed them and me. I was allowed to be one with them, to see practically all there was to be seen. I was told more than it is comfortable for me to know.

I felt, as far as my heart would let me, as they felt.

My tour of Africa started in London, in a basement office at 200 Gower Street, among the representatives of African student leagues and political committees. Then I wandered among the "Africa Houses" along Marble Arch and Warrington Crescent. There I found angry young Africans and their sympathizers filing endless indictments against colonialism and white domination. These young Africans will no doubt form the bulk of the ruling class once their lands receive independence, but they are far removed from the forces now at work to bring about the independence they will one day enjoy. Indeed, and this is a mark of the times, London, so long the refuge of assorted political exiles, including Africans, is now far removed from the forces contorting Africa. Only one of the responsible African politicians now on the brink of coming into their kingdoms maintains offices in London. The others have moved to Cairo, Accra, Conakry or back home.

Joshua Nkomo, the gentleman from Southern Rhodesia, was the last important politician to maintain offices on Gower Street. Early in 1960, Nkomo moved from Gower Street to a plush, two-story home-office along fashionable Golders Green Road. Nkomo is likely to be Prime Minister of Southern Rhodesia if the Central African Federation* breaks up and

* The Central African Federation consists of three British colonies: Southern Rhodesia, Northern Rhodesia and Nyasaland. The Federation came into being as a result of the European settlers' attempts to consolidate their political position against the rising tide of African nationalism. The Federation as a whole, of course, retains colonial status.

Southern Rhodesia receives independence. His credentials for that role are typical:

Nkomo was educated in Southern Rhodesia and then braved the racial winds while making his way through Adams College at Natal, South Africa. Upon returning home, Nkomo entered politics because he felt this was the most effective way for him to lodge a protest against racial conditions in his country. Nkomo came into his own in 1957 when he organized the African Nationalist Congress, an all-African political party. The settler government, leery of African political activity, raised opposition to the Congress. In 1958, Nkomo left Southern Rhodesia to attend the All-African Peoples Conference in Accra, Ghana, and the government seized the opportunity to move against his political party. The Congress was banned, all of Nkomo's lieutenants were thrown in jail. Nkomo never returned home. Instead, he moved to London and set up offices on Gower Street.

For the better part of two years, Nkomo played the freedom fighter's role. He wrote pamphlets, issued press releases, made his way to the platform of every "freedom" rally, joined with other freedom fighters in issuing an unending stream of propaganda calculated to turn world opinion against the white settlers and in favor of the Africans. At the invitation of the American Committee on Africa, Nkomo came to New York bringing with him the story of the hell that is Africa, Southern Rhodesia in particular. Like all effective freedom fighters, Nkomo mastered the art of inducing guilt in the hearts and souls of white people who have the money and power to change things. By 1960 the world climate was such that Nkomo decided on a bold move. At his signal, his lieutenants inside Southern Rhodesia—most of whom by then had been released from jail—organized the National Democratic party. Nkomo was named leader in exile. The settler government reacted instantly, then stopped short. Nkomo had done his work well. World opinion was against the settlers. The threat to arrest the leaders of the new political movement was withdrawn.

But Joshua Nkomo has done more than affect world opinion toward Southern Rhodesia during his two-year stint in London. He has managed to move from Gower Street to Golders Green Road, and that, by any yardstick, is quite a journey. As will shortly become evident, Nkomo's attractive home-office in Golders Green and improved conditions inside Southern Rhodesia are part and parcel of the same thing.

Mr. Nkomo received me flanked by two associates. One of them, Enoc Dumbushena, is a trained journalist and Nkomo's chief lieutenant in exile. The other, J. G. Silundika, is a member of the executive committee of the National Democratic party inside Southern Rhodesia and a member of the faculty of the University of Nyasaland and Rhodesia, at Salisbury. Silundika had come to London for talks with Nkomo, after which they both enplaned for the meeting of Independent African States, in Addis Ababa.

Forty-three-year-old Joshua Nkomo is a tall, heavy-set, dark brown man who relaxes quickly and talks easily. He reminded me of an American Negro Methodist clergyman I once interviewed just before he announced his candidacy for the bishopric.

"This is the situation in Southern Rhodesia," Nkomo began. "There are three million Africans as over against two hundred thousand white settlers. Only seventy thousand of the settlers vote and the property qualifications for voting are such that all but a few hundred Africans are prevented from voting."

How do you propose to change this?

"Well, as you know, we are a part of that damn Federation. We have to get rid of that first. Hastings Banda is carrying the load in Nyasaland, Kenneth Kaunda in Northern Rhodesia, and between the three of us we hope to topple the Federation within a year or so. This done, we can move for independence."

Do you think the Africans of the Federation can win their independence without violence?

"Almost certainly, yes. Violence, in our case, is becoming less and less of a probability. Our propaganda has been effective. African nationalism has been accepted by most of the world as one of the realities of modern life. I am all but certain that Southern Rhodesia can be liberated without violence. But the cases of our brothers in South Africa, Angola, Mozambique and one or two other places is quite another matter."

Are you saying the problems of these countries will be resolved in violence?

"Under the present circumstances, I see no other solution."

Once Southern Rhodesia is free, will you, as a probable Prime Minister, lend your good offices to freedom fighters who want to launch revolts against their governments?

"It would be indelicate of me to answer at this time. Why don't you just say the Rhodesias will soon be freed. Make a good report of that and when we are free, come around and we'll talk to you about if and how we plan to help our brothers in South Africa and some other places."

Is the white man welcome to stay in Africa, Southern Rhodesia, particularly?

"Why not? The white man can stay in Africa if he behaves himself!"

What do you mean by "if he behaves himself"?

At this point Dumbushena broke in to reply: "The white man can stay in Africa if he accepts the fact that he is just like the rest of us. He must not ask for unusual privileges."

"That is the way we feel," Silundika added. "Just before I left home we had a meeting on this. There is a role for the white man in Africa if he wants to become a citizen, not a lord and master. But they don't want that. If they can't rule us they will do as the French did in Guinea last year, pull down the telephone wires, haul off everything they can steal, and leave the country, hoping it will collapse."

There are constant reports that Christianity is losing out in Africa. Is this true?

"I am in the thick of it and I can tell you it is true," Silundika said. "The Church has not played a proper role in African affairs. It has stood against us, with those who would enslave us. The Church is on its last leg in Africa."

Are you, Mr. Silundika, a Christian?

"Yes. I am a Catholic. I was educated at Marian Hill College in Natal, South Africa. That's a Catholic school. The Church let me down. Of course, I didn't join the Church for political reasons. I joined out of spiritual convictions. Even so, I feel let down, badly so. Islam will win in Africa. And although I will remain a Catholic, I cannot honestly say that I am sorry about the turn of events. After all, religion is a vital part of a man's scheme of values. It should, if it would make a man of him, drive him toward freedom. This is where Christianity has failed. It gave us everything but freedom."

"Amen to that," Nkomo added.

Would you say "amen" to Communism?

Joshua Nkomo tensed. His brown eyes drew narrow, almost to bead points. Then he leaned forward in his chair, rested his elbows on the desk and proceeded to explode.

"We are not dying for economic ideologies. We are dying for freedom!"

I let quiet come back to the room before continuing.

But where do you stand in the East-West struggle?

"To quote Sekou Touré, 'East and West are not the only two poles. There are also North and South.' We are not going to get in this mad rush to nowhere," Nkomo continued, pounding away at the desk. Then he began to pat his hand on the desk while talking in cadence. "Nonalignment . . . nonalignment, nonalignment, positive neutrality . . . Call . . . it . . . what . . . you . . . will, we are not going to die for economic ideologies!"

Will you accept aid from the Russians?

"We will take help—money and arms, if necessary—from the East. After all the Allies thought nothing of accepting help from the Russians when they were closing in on Berlin. If the West doesn't want us to take help from the East, then why don't they give us aid?"

Assuming the West did give you aid, would you still accept help from the East?

"Yes. Whoever wants to help us, let him do so."

Speaking of aid, Mr. Nkomo, how does the freedom fighter live? How did you finance the move from Gower Street to Golders Green Road?

"The days of the ragged and hungry freedom fighter are over. If a man is a legitimate representative of the struggle in his country he can get help. There are three organizations —the All-African Peoples Conference, the Afro-Asian Solidarity Conference, and the Conference of Independent African States—they will see to it that a responsible freedom fighter sets up shop and gets his message told. Now, once a man is established," Nkomo continued, "he can do several things to aid himself and his cause. There are several non-African organizations in England and in the United States that will give aid if the man is legitimate."

Several people have told me that European businessmen offer freedom fighters tempting gifts and loans against the day when the Africans will be in power and can return the favors in terms of trade agreements and mineral rights. Is there any truth in this?

"Let me put it this way: The freedom fighter must be very careful. Once he is established, he is approached by all kinds of people. There is always somebody knocking on his door. Sometimes they come from the East, sometimes from the West; some of them represent private interests, others represent national interests. They all knock on the freedom fighter's door. He would do well to think before opening his door. I would suggest that you go deeper into this matter of money when you get to Cairo. I think you will get a much better answer there than I can give you."

As Nkomo continued talking I remembered two interviews I had had earlier in the day. I had talked first with Commander Fox-Pitt, head of the Anti-Slavery Society, and then with the Reverend Michael Scott, once a missionary, then a pleader for African causes before world councils and now head of London's Africa Bureau. These are white men, life-long friends of the Africans. They spoke for the Africans when the Africans could not speak for themselves. The Africans have now moved to the center of the stage and speak for themselves, out of their own suffering and with innate authority. Such is the ache in the African's heart, the pain in his soul, that even his closest white friends are suspect, shunted aside, religiously kept out of the conferences that plot Africa's tomorrow. But men like Fox-Pitt and Michael Scott have found a new role for themselves: as the last of the white men to have any valid contact with the Africans, these men are working quietly, patiently and, I hope, effectively, to retrieve Africa from the brink of racism. "I stay as close to them as I can," Michael Scott told me. "I just hope they don't learn to hate before we white people learn to love."

That night I began to feel as well as understand what the Reverend Mr. Scott had said. Diana Hermans, secretary to Fox-Pitt, arranged for me to meet the African writer William ("Bloke") Modisane. Diana and I went to Modisane's third-story flat along Park Hill Road together and we were received by Bloke and Elizabeth Morton, who, like Diana, is a South African white woman. Elizabeth's true name cannot be revealed here because she is a London schoolteacher and would lose her job if it were disclosed that she associated with an African. Indeed, Diana had just been evicted from her apartment because, as the landlord put it, "you have too many black visitors!"

What a field day American segregationists and South African followers of apartheid would have had if they had crashed that party! There we sat, an American Negro and a black South African, both of us writers, both of us married, flanked by two white women from South Africa.

Yet how wrong our critics would have been. I was in search of a story; nothing more. Diana and Elizabeth, like scores of other white South Africans in Europe and England, are trying to save their country. They say apartheid is wrong. They stand with the African, and want to work with the Africans to erect a government and way of life that will endure.

I had read Bloke's articles in *The Saturday Review* and *The New Statesman* and was shocked by the misery disclosed in the film *Come Back Africa,* in which he appeared as one of the African intellectuals who chided white liberals. Like the hero of the film Bloke spent most of his thirty-six years in Sophiatown, an African location just outside Johannesburg. Like the hero of the film, Bloke has been arrested by South African police because he violated the pass law. As was the film hero's wife, Bloke's father was killed by an African bandit.

"This you will never believe," Bloke said to me, "but I was educated by—of all people, and get this—*the Dutch Reformed Church!*" Although Diana and Elizabeth had heard the story before, they joined Bloke and me in ironic laughter.

But the humor was short-lived.

"You Negroes made it by going to court," Bloke said to me. "But we Bantu will have to do it another way. The law is with you American chaps, but it is against us in South Africa."

"How will you do it?" I asked.

"That is yet to be decided. By 1963—the deadline set by the Pan-African Congress*—it will all be over."

* The African political party which organized the recent revolt against the pass laws in South Africa.

"How about guns?"

"Such things are always available if one really wants them."

"How about your white friends in South Africa? Men like Alan Paton. What will happen to them?"

"We appreciate all they have done," Bloke said. "We hope they take us seriously. No one wants to harm them."

"Are you a part of it?" I asked Bloke. "Will you fight when the time comes?"

"I am waiting for a phone call," Bloke said. "Thousands of us are waiting. I don't know when the call will come. I only know that it will come. That will be it. We will gather in an appointed country, and then go home to South Africa, never to leave again. We will govern unless they kill us. Either way, at long last the Bantu's soul will be at rest."

I looked up into the faces of Diana and Elizabeth. They were flushed with emotion. They knew Bloke was telling the truth. I, too, knew Bloke was telling the truth. I had seen irrefutable proof of what the South Africans had in mind before I left New York. The government of South Africa also knows. On May 29, 1960, the Johannesburg *Times* charged, "The black states of Africa and Egypt are joining in a vast plot against the Union of South Africa. Their aim is to destroy South Africa, by force if necessary, unless there is a change in the Union's racial policy." Perhaps this is why, at about the same time, the American government asked other nations to join her in an agreement not to sell arms to African rebels.

"What about Diana and Elizabeth?" I asked.

"That's just it," Elizabeth snapped. "If they only realized that we love South Africa as much as they do. It's our land as much as it is theirs. We love it and we love them. We are as much against racism as they are. Both Diana and I broke with our families because of racism. We hate it! We are willing to do anything to eliminate it. If they would only let us help!"

"No," Bloke said, "you cannot help. We must do it ourselves. Once the change is complete we can say to all, 'Come, live as one with us. And in the heat of the noonday sun, let us sit down—together!' "

I had heard all this before—not quite so eloquently, however—from dozens of Africans representing several countries. They really believe they can whip their mass followers to a frenzy against the white man, then make a U-turn and establish a state where all races can live together in harmony. Diana and Elizabeth don't believe it. I don't believe it either.

It was three o'clock in the morning when I climbed onto the back of Diana's motor scooter to be driven back to my hotel along Marble Arch. London was quiet and asleep. So typical of the secure Western world: shockingly unaware of the obvious.

Nkomo and Bloke Modisane, frankly, unnerved me. What bothered me most was the fact that Africans are totally unwilling to accept whites as coequals and partners in a free government, yet they have no qualms about accepting money from both East and West while saying, in effect, "A plague on both your houses."

My next stop should have been Cairo. Instead, I flew into Paris and had a long talk with Richard Wright, the expatriate American Negro writer. Richard has written three books on Africa and I wanted to check my impressions against his. An avowed ex-Communist, he shared my concerns. He told me of an instance in which he had been asked to act as go-between for an African politician on the brink of power and a certain "Eastern" businessman who was interested in obtaining mineral rights once the African led his land to independence. "I told them both," Richard said, "that I would not be a party to Africans prostituting themselves."

And as Richard continued talking I realized that somewhere, somehow he had become bitter toward the Africans. Part of the bitterness, it emerged, stemmed from the long-standing feud between Africans and American Negro intellectuals. "We gave birth to this African independence thing," Richard said, pointing first to himself and then to me. "This thing started with American Negroes—Du Bois and George Padmore. Then these Africans got high-handed and snobbish toward us." I knew something of what Richard was talking about. I have been in casual gatherings where American Negro intellectuals used the words "snobbish," "imperious" and "arrogant" when referring to Africans. Some years before we met, my wife dated an African. The incipient romance foundered when he informed her that he was doing her a favor by taking her out.

But all this was before the wind of change began to shake Africa. Now, according to the gospel of black brotherhood, we are all one—thanks to the white man's opprobrium.

"I'll be interested to hear what you find," Richard said as I left. "And keep your eye peeled for something I call 'dependency mentality.' "

I should have left Paris late that afternoon. I was already two days off schedule, and my anxiety concerning the truth about Africa had become an aching drive. Fate, aided by mechanical failure in an Air India jet, kept me in Paris for an additional fifteen hours. Even the surfeit of pleasure which is having a night in Paris at the expense of an airline failed to unknot my apprehensive soul, so concerned it was (and is now, but even more so) about what lay ahead. But as wise men know, fate often has reasons of its own.

It might not have happened had I not offered to help a fellow passenger with his cabin baggage. All I knew of him was that we were stranded for a night in Paris together. Then the personal facts began to emerge: my companion was Dr. Yehia el-Alily, perhaps the major real estate broker in Cairo. He had been on a business trip to New York and Chicago and then detoured into Zurich to visit his two sons in school there.

Dr. el-Alily was as white a man as I had ever encountered. His slight tan made him a dead ringer for a white resident of Miami Beach, Florida. Yet, as we talked, his jargon was that of the black brotherhood: what the white colonialists had done to "us." How "we" must move out on our own and do things without "them." "They" thought "we" couldn't do it but "we" showed "them." "General Gamal Abdel Nasser has taught 'us' black men to stand on our own feet."

It was the next day. The Air India jet was eight miles up, out over the Mediterranean somewhere between Sicily and Crete. Dr. el-Alily left his first-class seat to visit me in the tourist section. His soul was on fire with black brotherhood. There was no pretense in his presence, no patronizing desire to comfort me because I was colored. His conviction was consuming.

When we landed at that Cairo airport, Dr. el-Alily told the

officials who I was. They whisked me through customs (not one of my bags was touched) while the other sweating passengers were still waiting in the relentless heat. For the first time in my life I saw black (that is to say, nonwhite) airport officials, customs officers, airplane mechanics, bank officials. And, as has been the case everywhere else I've ever been, the menials were also black.

The airlines bus zipped out through the desert into town. The driver was silent—until we got to the edge of town, that is; then he turned into a chattering tourist guide.

"See that big house there," he told us. "Under Farouk, one man—one man, mind you—he live in all that big house. General Abdel Nasser take it away. Now we have it. Soldiers live there."

Outside the house in full uniform, steel-helmeted soldiers stood erect, their guns glittering in the sun, bayonets unsheathed.

Along block after block there was mansion after mansion, all once occupied by Farouk's sycophants and their concubines. Now, thanks to General Abdel Nasser, they were occupied by soldiers in the name of the people.

Then we stopped in the center of Cairo. It was not the airlines terminal.

"See that Diesel engine," the driver said, pointing to a store window. We craned our necks and there sat the engine in the showcase. Under the engine there was a sign, "Made in Egypt."

"Black man made that," the driver said. He sat quiet and worshiped for a moment. The white tourists reflected awkward curiosity. I smiled. Thanks to the sessions at the Red

Rooster I knew what it was all about.

After one day of meeting U.A.R. government officials I realized two things: Nasser has brought on both the Egyptianization and Africanization of Egypt. A stranger can hardly make his way about in Cairo; the English language street signs have all come down. Here and there an obscure English road sign can be found, but one dares not depend upon them. Taxi drivers, with rare exceptions, speak no English. Businessmen haggle in halting English, even then in terms of Egyptian pounds. In my hotel, in the gift shop, the post office, the open markets, civil servants drew me aside to talk about our common enemy, the white man. "What are you going to do about Little Rock? Mississippi? When are you American black men going to come and help us run the white man out of Africa?" These were the things asked of me. They had heard nothing good about America, or about any "white" country, for that matter.

They knew everything about Little Rock except who eventually won the argument. They had heard and read about the sit-ins, yet they did not know that most of the stores involved have integrated their lunch counters. The Egyptians recounted these events with great detail, with fervor, as if they had been there. I listened stoically, for I *had* been there. I saw all these violations against the dignity of black Americans: I felt them, I suffered them, I wrote and cried aloud about them. And so, like a youth who has been at the Saturday movies all day long, I wiggled in my seat waiting for the Egyptians to come to the last reel—you know, the part where the U.S. Attorney General erupts, troops march in with banners flying, tanks rumbling, and place the American government on the side of equality. But the Egyptian version of the American black man's ordeal never gets that far: In the gospel according to Cairo, black Pauline is still tied to the rails, the roaring train bears down on her saintly image, while the white-skinned villain cackles in the bush just beyond the trestle. Some Egyptians, of course, know the full truth about the American race problem. But my close Egyptian friends warned me not to argue back, not to tell the Egyptian masses the latest chapter in the American Negro's struggle with the white man. "If the word gets out that you in any way apologize for, or seek to explain, what is happening in your country, every door will be closed to you. You will find it impossible to get interviews. Nobody will come near you."

This was my first encounter with planned ignorance; half-truths, well calculated to condition the masses to die for whatever bold cause the state declares.

For four years, now, the U.A.R. press has handled every international story in a manner calculated to emphasize the colonialist role of European countries; America is pictured as their anti-black, imperialist co-conspirator. I arrived in Cairo two weeks after Nasser had nationalized the press. Veteran observers told me the anti-Western news slant was at its worst. Each morning the papers regurgitated the U-2 incident and the subsequent collapse of the Paris Summit Conference: every rehandling of the story was imbued with a new anti-Western tidbit. Yet, strangely enough, the treatment was not pro-Russian. Both East and West emerged from the columns of the U.A.R. press as wicked and inept powers, each determined to rule or ruin. This imminent danger stated, the press went on to venerate nonalignment. It was a timely harangue. President Nasser was visiting Yugoslavia's Marshal Tito; against the backdrop of the East-West conflict, the national press projected the two heads of state as the hope of the world.

There is more than meanness in Nasser's method: regardless of what one may think of his motivations, Nasser has given his people the deepest sense of national pride they have known since Biblical days. Justified or not, the Egyptian people believe in themselves, in their ability to create and accomplish without "white" help. Justified or not, the Egyptian people are convinced that nonalignment will, in the nick of time, save the world from racism and war. But there is more. The Egyptian people now look upon themselves as Africans. This is what I encountered in Dr. el-Alily. The same message leaped in big bold type from the front pages of every U.A.R. newspaper.

Nor does Nasser stop there. "We cannot stand aloof from the struggle now shaking Africa," he said in his *Philosophy of the Revolution*. Now the world knows that he meant it. The Nile forks at Cairo, and in Zamalek, a section of the island between the two branches, an imposing array of African freedom fighters sit in luxuriously furnished offices turning out protests against colonialism and white domination. Exiles from Uganda, Somali, Kenya, the Cameroons, Nigeria and Chad had offices in Cairo when I was there. In the six weeks since I left, exiles from South Africa, Southern Rhodesia, and Southwest Africa have also set up camp along the banks of the Nile. Late at night, Radio Cairo booms down into Africa in several dialects: "Freedom!" "Independence!" "Down with imperialism!" "Beware of Israel!"

Exiled Africans are special guests on these programs. This is how they flash signals back home; this is how the fire of freedom is kept burning against the day when independence will come. And it is in Egypt, not too far from Cairo, that the core of an international black army dedicated to the liberation of Africa is being formed.

Who pays for all this?

The three African organizations, the All-African Peoples Conference, the Conference of Independent African States and the Afro-Asian Solidarity Conference, maintain special funds for the support of Africans in exile. The money for this operation is held by the various secretariats, but several independent countries, Guinea, Ghana and the U.A.R. particularly, make separate direct contributions to African exiles.

To a man the freedom fighters in Egypt are "guests" of the U.A.R. government. This is their grubstake. Once they are in Cairo, thus certified as legitimate, the African exiles get overtures from both wings of the Communist bloc. They are invited to attend "student rallies" in Peking, "African seminars" in Moscow.

How do they get to Peking and Moscow?

I put the question to several freedom fighters and found that an honest-to-God African exile, particularly if he has been put in jail by the British, French or Belgians, can get an all-expense-paid trip to Moscow or Peking—usually both—plus three thousand dollars "personal money."

I asked one freedom fighter why he needed three thousand dollars in personal expenses.

"Well," he said in a clipped British accent, "one can't go to

Peking naked even though everybody in Peking is naked, can one?"

The impact of Russia and China on these exiles is cause for concern. They are not converted to Communism—they suspect it—but they are led to believe that the Communist governments are sympathetic to their cause while the Western governments are not. Thus they move onto the no-man's land of nonalignment and set out to finance their movements with money extracted from as many sources as possible.

The freedom fighters admire Nasser even if they do not trust him. They resent having their phones tapped, their mail censored. But this happens to everybody in Egypt. They think Nasser's stance as a black African is a bit strained, yet they cannot deny that, in a very real sense, the Egyptian people have come to feel one with the Africans. The gravest suspicion of Nasser stems from the fact that he harbors not only exiles moving against colonialism and white domination, but also those exiles fighting against African politicians in their home states. For example, the bitterest opposition to Kenya's Tom Mboya comes from two Kenya freedom fighters in Cairo. There is no bar against African politicians in Cairo and Mboya has quite a lively African opposition there. The Kenyans in Cairo are "Nasserites," men who oppose Mboya because he allegedly has accepted "Jewish" money. A similar situation exists with respect to the Cameroons. Nasser, along with Ghana's Nkrumah, gives open financial and moral support to Dr. Roland Moumie, leader of the revolt against the African government in the Cameroons.

Beyond all this, however, there is an extremely personal dimension to this Nasser operation. Freedom fighting is lonely business. African exiles find themselves thousands of miles away from home, parted from their families, friends, the traditions they loved so deeply. In time, these men develop roots in Egypt. The result is a human bond which will stand Nasser and the U.A.R. in good stead once these men bring independence to their lands. Take the case of Ali O. Senyonga, the Cairo representative of the Uganda National Congress, for example. Senyonga is twenty-six years old. He has been in Cairo five years. During the lonely nights he attended school, mastered the difficult Arabic language. Then he entered the University of Cairo. In between fighting for Uganda's independence Senyonga fell in love with an Egyptian girl. Radiantly in love, they received me together in his plush office in Zamalek. Now, what does Senyonga do in the Cairo office of the Uganda National Congress? When I was in Cairo, Senyonga was second in command to John Kale, a likely candidate for Prime Minister of Uganda. Since I have returned home, Kale was killed in an airplane crash while en route to Moscow, where he was to have been the Soviet Union's guest for the Powers trial. Specifically, Senyonga was —and still is—in charge of obtaining scholarships for students from Uganda. For the year 1959-60, Senyonga placed thirty students in the University of Cairo; his fifteen other charges are scattered in France, England, Russia, China and the United States. One day Uganda will be independent. Ali Senyonga will be in the forefront of the ruling class; he will be joined by the university graduates whom he personally placed. At the center of their gratitude will be Nasser and Egypt, a man and a land who stood *in loco parentis* during their time of trouble. This is futuristic and personal diplomacy at its best. What Nasser has done is to win these, and scores of other, Africans over to him and to Egypt.

This was the pattern wherever I went among the Africans in Egypt: the Kenyans, the Somali—most black Africans—speak of Nasser from their hearts rather than their heads. They know and see his faults. Yet they see him as a brother. To a man they have sat in his office and had tea; to a man they have opened their hearts to him and said they were hungry, oppressed children a long way from home; to a man they will tell you that Nasser fed and clothed them, that he ordered his government to give them lavish offices in mansions once lived in by Farouk's chosen few. Nasser created a forum where these men met the Russians and Chinese, who spend money like water in the hope that one day the water will turn to manganese, gold and cobalt. Both Nasser and his African children smile at this because they know that nonalignment is as far as they are going. They sit back and let the East and West and China fight over them: the only winners will be the nonaligned. This is how they propose to build their dams, smelt their ore, dig their diamonds, mine their gold, sell their cobalt, push their manganese, grow their cotton, fight their wars, feather their own bourgeois nests and free their people.

The man behind this vast "Africanization" operation is a disarmingly nice fellow, Murse Saad el-Dine. Like most educated Egyptians, Murse's credits are longer than his years. He is thirty-seven and he holds a B.A. in English from Cairo University, a B.S. from the London School of Economics and a Ph.D. in philology from London University. Characteristically enough, Murse wrote his doctoral dissertation on "The Language of Humor." In addition to being book censor for the U.A.R. government (no book appears on

Egyptian book stalls until Murse's personal recommendation has been approved by General Nasser), Murse lectures on languages at Cairo and Ainshams universities. He is technical adviser to the government's Bureau of Arts and Literature, and he is in charge of press, radio and TV for the National Union, Nasser's new amorphous political party. These are Murse's government jobs. The list of his civilian posts is much longer.

"I know you think I have too many jobs, Louis," Murse said to me, "but we don't have the reservoir of trained men you have in America. The only way Egyptians can run Egypt is for every educated Egyptian to double or triple in many jobs. This is our answer to the white man's charge that we don't have enough educated men to run our government. In time we will have enough trained people and I can give up some of my jobs."

Murse was the only man I met in Egypt who was willing to criticize Nasser.

"I am not satisfied with the support President Nasser is giving to the boycott of South Africa," Murse said flatly, "and when he gets back from Yugoslavia I'm going to see him about it."

If any man has earned the right to be bumptious toward Nasser on the African question, Murse has: Russia was boiling mad because their representatives were left out of the Afro-Asian States Conference at Bandung, in 1955. New Delhi Communists took up the cause, arguing that Russia properly belonged at the conference because fourteen of the U.S.S.R.'s provinces lie inside Asia. These were the days during which Nasser and Russia were going steady and Nasser received a "good will mission" seeking to bring on the formation of an

Afro-Asian organization that would include Russia. As a result, the first Afro-Asian Peoples Conference was held in Cairo on December 27, 1957.

"Let's face it," Murse said to me, "the Communists dominated the conference."

Even more than that, the conference gave the Russians a "brother" relationship with the Africans, something they never had before. Once one remembers how close Africa is to tribalism, how unguarded and outgoing they can be once they feel they are among their own, the sheer psychological advantage of the Afro-Asian Peoples Conference becomes evident. By no stretch of the imagination or of ethnic kinship could the West share in that togetherness. As a result, all of the pro-Western African and Asian states boycotted the conference.

Then came the break between Russia and Egypt. Although Yousef el-Sebai, Egypt's best-known writer, had been named Secretary General of the Afro-Asian Peoples Conference, Murse Saad el-Dine, second in command of the Secretariat, was assigned to wrench the conference from Communist hands. Thereupon the Russians got an elementary lesson in African politics. First off, Murse went to work on the pro-Western nations—Liberia, Ethiopia, Iran, Pakistan, Turkey and the Philippines. Murse convinced the Liberians that Nasser was out to slay the Communists at the next meeting and that he needed their help. The Liberians agreed to come. Then, employing the same argument, Murse persuaded the Ethiopians to attend with the understanding that Ethiopia's touchy situation with Eritrea would not be discussed. This done, Murse "arranged" for the Secretariat to get an invitation from Sekou Touré asking that the second Afro-Asian

Peoples Conference meet in Conakry, the capital of Guinea. This invitation was placed before the executive committee along with a year-old invitation from behind the Iron Curtain. Before the Communists realized what had happened the committee had voted to meet in Conakry. The Conakry meeting was opened by Sekou Touré himself; he took that occasion to deliver his strongest nonalignment speech to date. The delegates roared their approval, neutralism won the day, leaving the Russians and Chinese mumbling to themselves.

"The West will fail in Africa," Murse said, recovering from his hilarity over his defeat of the Communists at Conakry. "But don't pay too much attention to this talk about Christianity and Islam fighting it out in Africa. Islam will make some gains, but neither of them will really win Africa." I could not discount this view, coming, as it did, from one of Nasser's trusted servants, a devout Moslem, and a most knowledgeable man about African affairs.

"You American Christians have misread us," Murse continued. "Nasser never desired to win Africa for Islam. Rather, we see the wisdom of a free and friendly Africa. We are not out to make Moslems of Africans. We are out to make friends for Egypt. Beyond this, we do have a genuine interest in the problems of oppressed peoples. We are all black brothers. This goes beyond Islam. Now, of course, if black men look up one day and realize that followers of Islam freed them and they turn toward Mecca . . . well, that's something else again."

Are you consciously seeking to carve out a color bloc?

"No," Murse said. "Not really. Like the question of Africa going Islamic, that could be the end result. Here is what General Abdel Nasser is saying and doing: One, we are against imperialism in all forms; two, we don't want any foreign bases in Africa or Asia—let them blow up their own countries, not ours; three, there must be no atom tests anywhere in Asia or Africa; four, every African and Asian country must be given independence *now;* five, white domination must be ended in Africa and Asia at all costs. There is nothing we will not do to bring this about."

Is it true that your government supports African freedom fighters here in Cairo?

"Yes. I can't say just how it is all arranged. These matters are worked out between President Gamal Abdel Nasser and the Africans individually."

Would I be correct in saying that each freedom fighter works out his own deal with your President?

"That, as far as I know, is true."

Does this account for the fact that some African freedom fighters have luxurious offices while others, the Nigerians for example, work in what one might call Spartan quarters?

"That's a valid analysis. The relationship between President Nasser and the Africans is a very personal one. The details are worked out at that level. Like you Americans, we Egyptians are apt to be kinder toward those who agree with us than we are toward those who have reservations about our over-all plans."

Murse, what about reports that Africans accept money from the Russians and Chinese? I don't mean African countries already free. Rather, I'm speaking of African politicians in exile.

"This is true. I was a little worried about the way the Chinese, particularly, were wheeling and dealing at Conakry. Money flowed like water. I warned some of the Africans about getting in over their heads. But this is up to them."

Does your government deny that it completely finances Radio Cairo and that it supports whatever line Radio Cairo lays down?

"Let's put it this way. All radio stations in the United Arab Republic are under government control. We know what's going on. Let's be candid about it," Murse said. "Radio Cairo is our best weapon against Israel. This is how we tell the Africans to beware of Jewish money."

After my interview with Murse, I had lunch with Morey Atamley, the Russian member of the executive committee of the Afro-Asian Solidarity Conference. Atamley, a pleasant fellow in his late twenties, confirmed all I had been told about Russia's efforts to win African support. He responded good-naturedly when I needled him about the turn of events at Conakry.

"Yes," he said, "things were touch and go between Russia and the U.A.R. for a while. But Murse and I never wavered in our personal friendship."

Then, over coffee, Atamley lapsed into brooding silence. I could feel it, yet there was nothing I could do about it. Like most Russians in Africa, Atamley was consumed by awkwardness. Nasser had allowed them to be black men for a brief and rewarding hour; then the Russians fouled the Arab's nest by demanding more than he was willing to give. And Nasser gave them the back of his hand. He still allows them to sow seed in Africa's fertile land, but through ways which he alone fully understands Nasser sees to it that the Russians reap less and less.

"Pardon me," the waiter said, interrupting my last words with the Russian. "There is a telephone call for you."

My plane companion, Dr. el-Alily, was on the other end of the wire. Would I be so kind as to address the Cairo Rotary Club at noon on the following day?

I would.

As I sat on the dais in the grand ballroom of the Nile Hilton, I remembered Gertrude Stein's caustic remark that Hemingway was a Rotarian at heart. I wondered if I, too, was but another happy-go-lucky huckster of the *status quo!*

For the most part, the Cairo Rotarians were colored men, about my complexion. The remainder were Syrians and Greeks—Egyptians and Africans all. There were some white men there, English and American businessmen, but they have long since reconciled themselves to being tolerated strangers.

I was something of a novelty. The Egyptians had seen Negro Americans before, of course, but most of them had been there under the aegis of the American State Department; they had been "apologists for the American white man." I later found out that the word had been passed that I was a "free" Negro; one who had not "sold out." The basis for this, I later discovered, was an article I wrote for the June, 1960, issue of *Harper's* in which I said Negro leadership was out of touch with mass feelings.

When the time came for me to speak I congratulated the Egyptians for having identified themselves with black men, their struggle and their cause. I told them that as a black man, an oppressed man, I gloried in their pride, their determination to prove that they could do things if allowed first to learn, then to act. Then I said Jews were people. Human beings. They, too, love life, have a right to all that it offers. The Cairo Rotarians sat in stony silence as I asked that they extend the brotherhood to include everybody who believed in and lived for human freedom.

The first man to shake my hand after the speech was an American white man from North Carolina. He was in Cairo to seal a business deal. "By God," my fellow American said, "I don't agree with the sit-ins. But I guess you got it right. We all, black and white, got to live in this world together, and the sooner we get the hell on with it, the better off we all will be."

The Arabs reacted differently. They shook my hand, gave me their cards, invited me to dinner.

"*Ah lan wa sahlam,*" the brown-skinned public relations man for the Nile Hilton said. An Egyptian friend quickly translated. "You are here as a relative," I had been told. "You have entered into a peaceful place."

Later that day I received word that Kamal el-Malakh, feature editor of *Al Ahram,* the *New York Times* of Egypt, would like to interview me. Would I come to lunch the following day at the Sportsman's Club in Zamalek?

"When the British were here," Kamal said to me, pointing out toward the vast green surrounding the Sportsman's Club, "neither you nor I could come here. Now we can come. The club is ours. The Europeans come here if they want to, but they must sit beside black men. If they don't want to do this they can stay home."

As Kamal talked I thought of all the places I couldn't go, all the clubs I cannot belong to in America. I understood his moment of triumph.

"Who are some of the black Americans you admire?" Kamal asked me.

I mentioned every prominent Negro I could think of.
"What about Sammy Davis, Jr.?"
"He's a great entertainer," I replied.
"Quite controversial, isn't he?"
"Yes," I admitted. "Many people don't like him."

Under Kamal's questioning we reviewed the plight of black men all over the world, particularly in America. Time and time again Kamal reminded me that he was a member of the Sportsman's Club. The British were no longer in control. He was proud, and I was proud for him.

The next day *Al Ahram* hit the streets. Its feature page carried a two-column headline, "Black American Writer Visits Cairo." At the bottom of the article there was a small picture of me, beside it a picture of Kamal, the same size. Above us both, there was a huge picture of Sammy Davis Jr.; it was a half-profile with emphasis on his lips, eyes and nose.

"You are famous," Dr. Mohammed Aly Saib, a close friend who is also professor of engineering at the University of Cairo, chided me over the phone. "Your picture is in the paper."

"I only wish I knew what they said about me," I replied.
"Come to tea," he laughed, "and my wife and I will translate it for you."

I went to tea.

Mohammed translated the article with great relish. His wife, an Englishwoman who not only converted to Islam but spent some months in Cairo winning over Mohammed's parents before she married him, took the translation down in longhand.

Kamal's article was most flattering. It put me in the long line of black Americans who have made their marks in life: Marian Anderson, W. E. B. Du Bois, Paul Robeson, Jackie Robinson, Ralph Bunche, practically every prominent Negro of the past two decades.

Then, to my amazement, the article continued with this alleged exchange between me and Mr. el-Malakh:

"What do you think about Sammy Davis, the famous singer and the fiancé of the Swedish actress May Britt?"

"Well," I allegedly replied, "as a matter of fact I have to say that no brown person respects or likes him any more.

"Not because he changed his religion and became Jewish two years ago, not for that, because everyone has his own freedom to choose what faith he likes. But we dislike him because he tried to get closer and closer to the people who have power in the night clubs and also because he changed his face when he had plastic surgery performed in order to hide his wide nose. He wanted to lose his African look, as if he felt ashamed to be a brown person from Africa. For that reason he lost our good-will. We had all sympathized with him when he lost one of his eyes and had to have a glass one."

The legend under Sammy Davis's picture read:

"Sammy Davis tried to disguise his African heritage but the scars from the operation still show his real nose."

This was Nasser's Egypt. A strange and forced world of black men, not really black but feeling as if they are, who put their arms around and honor all things black and then douse them in all the hates that make Nasser run. Late into the night, that night, my phone rang. Egyptians who had met me casually, now that they had read Kamal's article, wanted to know me personally. The hotel servants smiled and bowed as I walked by on my way to breakfast the next morning. The shopkeepers cut their prices in half, now that they knew who I was, what I stood for. The prostitutes who infest the hotels, despite Nasser's efforts to clamp the lid on the flesh-pots, offered me special considerations.

It was too late, then, for me to say that I was not to be associated with what Kamal had written. Those who knew me knew what I felt. But for the Egyptians—and they alone mattered for the moment—Kamal's article had been the stamp of approval. I was in. The portals of black brotherhood swung open. All Brother Lomax had to do was keep his mouth shut.

"The things you have been through are very real," Raymond Barrett, political officer in charge of African affairs at the American Embassy in Cairo, told me. "This is what Nasser attempts to say and do to black men."

Then Ray, about as dedicated a foreign service officer as I have ever encountered, patiently retraced the steps I had taken toward understanding Nasser's thrust.

"The West is in trouble in Africa," Ray told me. "America is taking a licking. There is nothing we can do about it at the moment. Our alliances with France, England, Belgium and, as far as the U.A.R. is concerned, with Israel are something the Africans can never understand. They feel we are against them."

Turning to his major criticism of American efforts in Africa, Ray said: "The Voice of Cairo beams down into Africa in God knows how many languages. The people involved can understand what is being said. The Voice of America goes down into Africa in English and French. The masses can't understand what we are saying."

Ray had said about all his position as a State Department

official would allow him to say. Both he and I knew, however, that there was much more to the story. The remainder has to do with broadcast content: The Voice of Cairo roars down into Africa exhorting the masses to revolt against colonialism; by contrast, the Voice of America is limited to platitudes about human freedom, to interviews with American Negroes whose success stories the Voice of America hopes will impress Africans. Unfortunately, an African living under economic, political and social oppression is not interested in how well off American Negroes are. Such news only baffles him, makes him suspect America even more. For if the American Negro is well off, the Africans argued to me, "why don't they come help us?" The inference was all too clear: in the process of becoming well off, the American Negro, like the white man, had grown indifferent toward Africa.

I asked Ray if he felt Nasser's Afro-Asianism was a real threat to the West.

"In a sense," he replied. "Every shift to neutralism is a shift away from the West. This is our greatest threat at the moment. These meetings of the Afro-Asian Solidarity Conference and the All-African Peoples Conference amount to more on paper than they do in reality. Yet these resolutions, these denunciations of the West are things Africans, including Egyptians, want to hear.

"Now, let's examine what has happened in African countries that have gained their independence," Ray continued. "As a general matter, trade patterns have not changed. Our studies show that in Ghana, Somali and Togoland, there has been little or no economic defection. Economically, these countries are about as they were before independence. The major exception, of course, is Guinea. There the Chinese Communists have made tremendous inroads."

This was a State Department officer's way of saying that economic patterns don't change in countries where independence is achieved with a minimum of ill will. He did not say it, but as Ray spoke about the state of things in Guinea I knew he was remembering how the French ripped the telephones from the walls, carted off the furniture from Sekou Touré's office. With the help of the Communists, Guinea limped toward independence and now hobbles toward stability. And in African minds, the sins of the French are visited upon their American allies.

Listening to this argument and realizing that it came from white American State Department people, I felt the depth of their personal dedication and involvement. They sit laced to their swivel chairs watching the greatest freedom explosion in human history occur in an anti-American, antiwhite, anticapitalist, anti-Western context. They think they know what to do about it, but they cannot act. And this is the vast gulf between American pronouncements and African aspirations; the Africans know that once they cross into freedom and independence we will stand with them. But we cannot help them in the critical hour of the great crossing. Rather it is Nasser, Sekou Touré, Kwame Nkrumah, battle-scarred veterans of change, who openly and boldly lead the way. And with the birth of each independent African state the neutralist camp becomes larger than it has ever been before. This is how and why freedom and nonalignment have become one in African minds.

I chose to walk from Ray's office at the American Embassy in Garden City back to my hotel in the center of Cairo. There was so much for me to think and feel about. There is something dead, and ancient, and crumbling, and unchanging about Cairo. I could not bring myself to believe that new and promising concepts of human progress were being born there. Yet I could not go against the evidence.

The dynamics of Nasser's Egypt are elusive. On the surface —as one walks the streets of Cairo, takes off his shoes and wanders through El Ahazar University and its Moslem center, and then makes his way through the narrow streets of old Cairo, and as one shoos off the haggling salesmen and beggars who infest every inch of the byways—Egypt, the U.A.R. for that matter, is a dead thing. It simply doesn't appear to be going anywhere. Then somebody who knows takes you by the hand. He drives you to a newly paved city square. You wonder why. Then he tells you a story: One morning the powers that be decided this road should be repaved. An hour later a thousand men swung into action. The road was blocked off, traffic was rerouted. While some men worked, others went to fetch high-powered lamps. The work continued, day and night. In less than forty-eight hours after the decision was made, the road was completed. I wondered if the day would ever come when Robert Moses and Mayor Wagner and Hulan Jack could do this with a Manhattan street. Then my friend drove to the new "Electronics Center" jutting up along the banks of the Nile. By now all of Egypt's radio and TV stations have moved into the building. The mammoth structure was built and an entire radio-TV schedule put on the air in less than eighteen months from the time the decision was made to launch such a project. Later that day I sat in the office of a member of the faculty of Cairo University's School of Engineering and listened to him bargain with a couple of Germans who were being hired to give fifteen Egyptian students cram courses in German. The deal was consummated: the students embarked on a ten-day, eight-hours-a-day, German course and then enplaned for West Germany, where they would spend the summer getting practical experience in the world's best technical plants.

Then there is the Egyptian woman. For the most part she is still behind the veil, but a feminist revolution is already under way.

I saw it in Ghada Shabender, a reporter for *Al Ahram.* Ghada, now in her mid-thirties, is a gracious woman and a sensitive reporter. Her mind and spirit, however, bear scars inflicted by the barbs that daily prick any unmarried Moslem woman her age. But Ghada is a proud rebel, her family is a family of rebels: Dr. Rahman Shabender, Ghada's father, was the celebrated Syrian hero who fought the French to a standstill and then died at the hands of a paid assassin. Madame Sahrrah Shabender, Ghada's proud and aging mother, lived again her youth while telling me how she shocked Syrian society in the twenties by taking off her veil. Ghada's sister, Madame Sahab Halbouni, continued the tradition by marrying a boy she had known and been close friends with since she was an infant.

Little wonder, then, that Ghada flatly refused to play the traditional role of the sweet young Moslem thing who knew nothing of her future husband until the respective families had haggled over price and other cumbersome arrangements.

"I don't know when I became a rebel," Ghada said to me. "I sat at home for fourteen years after I finished high school.

I went to teas, made the right dances, was received by the right families. Eligible men sent me their cards but I could never bring myself to accept an arranged marriage. How can you love a man you do not know?" she asked. Then, answering her own argument, she continued. "In our society it is assumed that a girl should allow her family to make a good match, that love will follow. But it does not always follow. I know many young women, schoolmates of mine, who are miserable. Their marriages are unhappy; their husbands take advantage of the laws of our faith and have more than one wife. If people knew each other first, and if they were in love, this could not be."

Ghada is among the new generation of Egyptian women who evoked horror from the conservatives when they went to work as waitresses in the lunchroom of the Nile Hilton. They pounded on Nasser's door until he gave them jobs as fare collectors on city buses. Then one night, on the dark route leading out to the Pyramids, the inevitable rape occurred. Amid a public storm, the feminists withdrew from the buses. The withdrawal, however, was to other fronts and they are skipping over the traces wherever and whenever they can. This feminist revolt has not hit black Africa yet. There are stirrings in Ghana, Guinea and Ethiopia, but for the most part, the African women are still loaded down with babies and firewood. One day the revolt will spread to them. And when it does, such Arab women as Ghada Shabender will stream down into Africa to help and applaud their sisters along the way. And another tie will bind Nasser to Africa, African to Nasser.

On my last Friday in Cairo, Ghada defied convention and went with me to lunch. After lunch we went shopping, buying dress material for my wife. That night I attended the graduation ceremonies at the American College for Girls as Ghada's guest. As we walked down the aisle to our seats, Egyptian dowagers craned their necks, their eyes bugged, some of them shook their heads disapprovingly, not because I am married (they accept polygamy) but because custom says an Egyptian girl cannot appear in public with a man until they are married. Ghada did not care, nor did her girl friends whom she had invited to meet me.

The sprawling green to the west of the college had been turned into an amphitheater. It was here, on this same green, that Billy Graham, at Nasser's leave, had brought Jesus to the Egyptians. But Billy Graham's appearance was a special dispensation. The American College, long Cairo's most elite school for girls and the American missionaries' best stand in Egypt, has long since been forbidden to teach religion. By law they are limited to the three R's, and word is that there are spies in every classroom to make sure the teachers keep within their limitations. The American missionaries had no choice. They could either quit preaching Christianity or go home. They chose to stay.

The graduates marched onto the stage to the rhythm of Mendelssohn's "March of the Priests." Then a Christian clergyman gave the invocation. While doting parents beamed, graduates rose and gave essays in French, English and Arabic. Then the college chorus sang "Unity of the Arab People."

Dr. Abd el Aziz el Sayed, Director of Education for the North Zone of the United Arab Republic, gave the address. First, Dr. Sayed brought greetings from General Gamal Abdel Nasser. Then he congratulated the graduates, exhorting them to take the lead in lifting the veil from the Arab woman's face. Ghada and her cohorts smiled. As they already knew, Nasser was solidly behind them.

Turning to the international scene, Dr. Sayed said: "We here in the United Arab Republic are neither exporting nor importing culture. Our way of life is our own."

Mrs. G. Frederick Reinhardt, wife of the American Ambassador, presented the prizes; His Excellency the Ambassador presented the diplomas. Then we all stood silent while the pianist played "The Star Spangled Banner." Following that, and with uplifted voices, the assemblage belted out the national anthem of the United Arab Republic, "My God Is My Armor."

Ghada is an alumna of the American College and she and I were permitted to attend the graduates' dinner that followed. I was introduced to Dr. Sarah B. Meloy, principal of the college. Dr. Meloy knew who I was and she was glad to have me there until I asked her, "Where do America and Christianity go from here?" As politely as possible, Dr. Meloy walked away. I don't blame her. Like Churchill, she had not come to Egypt to preside over the destruction of everything she believed in and stood for. Yet that is exactly what has happened.

I sat pensive as Ghada and I rode the bus toward her home. There was a smirk on her face. She knew that I, as any American Christian would be, was shaken by what I had seen. I was oblivious to the swarming crowd of men and women loaded down with babies who packed the bus. The bus lunged forward. A woman, her infant child strapped to her back, stumbled and fell almost the length of the bus. As amused fellow passengers lifted her to her feet, the woman shouted, "*Ha yba' zahma aktar fi Maka!*" Ghada, along with the other passengers, roared with laughter.

"Know what she said?" Ghada asked me.

"No," I admitted. "What?"

"She said," Ghada managed, still laughing, " 'We may as well get used to it for things will be much more crowded on the road to Mecca.' "

If Nasser's dream for the Moslem world comes true, the road to Mecca will, indeed, be crowded. Most observers believe it will not. Nasser's dream of Moslem unity—as well as his dream of Arab unity—has turned into a nightmare. Other Arab and Moslem leaders simply refuse to unite with Nasser, choosing rather to build small Arab and Moslem states of their own. Only Nasser's dream of a united Africa remains alive. And if Nasser continues to project himself as leader of the African world, this dream will also fade should Sekou Touré and Nkrumah have their way.

French West Africa, the Gold Coast, Sudan and Nigeria were able to move toward independence without bitter racial overtones because the Africans had clear title to their land once colonialism had been abolished. However, in some parts of Africa, notably Algeria and many countries south of the Sahara, large white settlements augmented by Asians raise infinitely complex and explosive questions. The moral issue aside, it cannot be doubted that the white settlers of Kenya, the Rhodesias, Angola, Mozambique and Nyasaland hold political as well as economic dominance. This is precisely why the Africans of the Central African Federation elected to stay under colonial rule until they could make certain that independence would catapult them, not the settlers, into political power. South Africa—along with its disputed mandate, Southwest Africa—is the exception that galvanizes the rule; for all practical purposes, these are European countries.

There is yet another facet of the decisive struggle now taking shape in Africa South: in the freedom timetable, it occurs eight years after the Egyptian revolution, four years after Ghana gained her independence, and two years after Guinea said "*non*" to the French proposition. Africans have now taken over their own affairs, replacing white missionaries as spokesmen for African independence before world councils. As a result, all of free Africa is reinvolved in the Africa South struggle, both as catalysts and as brothers. And the highly financed, well-oiled and sometimes crassly conducted campaigns to woo yet oppressed Africans into certain spheres of political influence affects the already independent African states as well.

The extent of this reinvolvement was clearly evident at the Second Conference of Independent African States, which met in Addis Ababa from June 14 through the 26th, 1960. After a round of "nonalignment" plenary speeches, the delegates spent most of the first week hearing complaints from representatives of African political parties in states still under colonialism and white domination. Meeting as committees and behind closed doors, the delegates adopted a series of resolutions (all of which are binding on their member states) that created a functional economic unity between all of the independent states, and which obligated these states, collectively and individually, to step up their intervention in the affairs of still colonialized states.

The degree to which the independent states are already

intervening in the affairs of "unfree" states mitigates against dismissing these resolutions as just so much political hot air. The quiet and almost completely unpublished implementation of such resolutions as these has moved Africa to the brink of an extremely serious explosion. For example, the delegates to the All-African Peoples Conference in Tunis on January 25, 1960, voted to ask the independent states to "allow" volunteers to train for service in Algeria. Three months later, the delegates to the Afro-Asian Solidarity Conference in Conakry, Guinea, adopted the same resolution. The conference almost panicked when the Chinese Communists took the floor and pledged to send one hundred thousand "technicians," veterans of Mao's "long march," any time the Algerian provisional government requested them. Both the All-African Peoples Conference and the Afro-Asian Solidarity Conference are nongovernmental organizations and there was a general tendency, particularly in the West, to laugh off the resolutions.

But on the day I arrived in Addis, Europe and Africa were swept by a report that Ghana volunteers were training in Ghana for service in Algeria. In private interviews both Mr. Omar Fanon, Algerian representative to the government of Ghana, and Mr. Frazer D. Ntem, press officer for the Ghana Ministry of Foreign Affairs, admitted to me that upwards of one thousand troops are training in Ghana, and that the volunteers will be pressed into service if needed. I received reliable but unconfirmed reports that volunteers for service in Algeria are also training in Guinea and the United Arab Republic. Several delegates to the Addis conference told me they were certain that the existence of these volunteer units had a direct bearing on General de Gaulle's decision to reopen talks with the Algerian provisional government.

In a scathing resolution, the delegates voted an economic boycott against South Africa that will prevent South African goods from being sold anywhere in Africa north of Angola; South African ships will no longer be permitted to call at ports operated by any of the independent states; planes owned or operated by South African airlines are denied access to landing facilities within the independent states and are also forbidden to "use the air space over member independent states." Going further, the delegates called on the Arab states to hold talks with petroleum companies for the purpose of halting the sale of petroleum to South Africa and to deny any concessions whatsoever to petroleum companies that continue to do business with the apartheid-ridden state.

"When we vote economic sanctions against these colonial states and demand that they change their political policies, we do not consider ourselves as intervening in the affairs of sovereign states," His Excellency Jamal Mohamed Ahmed, Sudanese Ambassador to Ethiopia, told me. "These Europeans have no rights whatsoever here in Africa. They are interlopers. We would never take such action against an independent African state."

The same taunt, set in the language of international politics, appeared in Tunisian Ambassador Taieb Slim's main address to the conference. Said Ambassador Slim: "Our relationship with the West is still based on great friendship and a common faith in a certain concept of freedom and individual rights. However, we blame them for being unwilling to renounce colonialism and, in the case of some of them, for not abandoning their open or tacit solidarity with the colonial powers. Before it is too late, we appeal to them sincerely to give up their colonialist mentality and dangerous complicity."

Most newsmen predicted that the resolution against South Africa would never be implemented. Now they know how wrong they were. Every independent African state has voted a total boycott against the Union. Nasser has denied South Africa access to everything but the Suez Canal. Going the resolution one better, Ghana not only has denied South African airways the rights set out in the resolution but now demands that every airline touching down in Ghana present a list of the South African citizens on board. Each South African passenger must then sign a sworn statement saying he is against apartheid. This could all but destroy Pan-American's South African service.

I underscore this because in Addis I detected a tendency by the world press not to take African politicians seriously. Africans themselves were the first to draw me aside and warn me against being influenced by what they called the "unsympathetic and disaster-wishing white press." I was not the only reporter disturbed by this. Colin Legum, of the London *Observer*, and Douglas Willis, of the BBC's Nairobi office, were seriously impressed by the behind-the-scenes moves at Addis. Legum, Willis and I were among the six correspondents chosen by the press corps to question Emperor Haile Selassie at an "open" palace press conference. Later, Legum remarked to me that this was the "most magnificent and statesmanlike African meeting I have ever seen." Willis felt the meeting would have grave repercussions and said so.

As I moved among the African politicians I found them affable but tense. Even when their talk is free, they are consumed by the history they feel sure they are making. Over cocktails they discuss Nasser's "three worlds" concept of Africa; gathered in a small section of the Ethiopian exhibition, they talk about Sekou Touré's recent book, *The Guinea Experience.* In M. W. K. Chiume, the gentleman from Nyasaland and the man who did the grass-roots work that put Hastings Banda in power, the African politicians have their acid wit. Said Chiume: "Why should Africans delay their freedom just because the white tribes of Europe are fighting among themselves?"

When asked why his brief case was so worn, Chiume is alleged to have retorted, "If you were as full of sedition as this brief case, you would be ragged about the edges also."

But it is during just such relaxed moments as these that one sees the other side of the African politician, the extremely personal and national sensitivity that results in international crises.

I encountered this African sensitivity during a party given by His Excellency A. M. Ribeiro, the Ghanan Ambassador to Ethiopia. I was seated at a table with the ambassadors from the United Arab Republic and Haiti, and their wives, along with the Ethiopian Foreign Minister, Mr. Yilma Deressa, and Mrs. Deressa. The conversation was light; for the better part of an hour we had been involved in a rather humorous discussion on the function of women in our respective cultures. Then suddenly His Excellency Dr. Ako Adjei, Ghana's foreign minister, walked over and took a seat among us.

"This is what Lumumba should do," Dr. Ako Adjei said, taking immediate charge of the conversation. "He should put all of the members of his opposition in jail the moment he comes to power!" A shocked silence fell over the table. "When Lumumba was getting ready to run for office he visited us in Ghana. I talked to him at length. Then, when the Congo elections came down to the wire, I went to Léopoldville and gave him on-the-spot guidance. I told him then he would have to arrest all those ambitious little men who were upsetting the applecart."

Then Dr. Adjei pointed his finger at me. "I know you don't like this," he said accusingly. "You American newsmen, black and white both, are all alike. You are always ready to accuse us of failing to practice democracy in Africa when you don't practice it yourselves. Democracy didn't work for you and it will not work for us. You know it will not work and you use it to try and sow discord in our African governments.

"If you people are so interested in Africa, then why don't you help us?" he demanded. "Your Mr. Dulles wouldn't loan us the money for the Aswan Dam, but we got it! You wouldn't loan us money for the Volta River Dam, but we got that too. You see," Dr. Adjei laughed, "we don't need you Americans any more."

Then, as if transformed by magic, the other people at the table, men and women, began to bore in on me. In their eyes I became America; they began to pelt me personally with all the grievances, real and imagined, they held against the United States.

The assault lasted for more than half an hour. As soon as one prosecutor—that's what they seemed like to me—stopped talking, another took up the cudgels. I felt embarrassingly defensive. I comforted myself by remembering that this was the kind of anti-American tirade many Americans have had to endure. The race question, the U-2, the Paris Summit blow-up, the Korean crisis, the wild mobs in Japan, the fall of the Turkish government, bit by bit these news fragments were fitted into an argument designed to prove that America was anticolored and in league with the "imperialist, colonialist powers."

I forgot myself and began to fight back. I said that I personally did not agree with all of the decisions made by the State Department, that I was both disturbed and embarrassed by the U-2 incident. I predicted that these issues would come up for mass judgment during the Presidential elections. This was a mistake: as my friends at the Red Rooster and in Cairo had warned me, any efforts on my part to defend America or even explain it would subject me to personal abuse.

"Another apologist for the white capitalists and colonialists," Dr. Adjei shouted, pointing his finger at me. "But the world knows what America is. Her record is scorched in the soul of every nonwhite man on the face of the earth."

Dr. Adjei's shouts attracted several dancers from the floor. They gathered around our table to hear what it was all about. Realizing he had an audience, Dr. Adjei really let go.

"Tell you what," he said magnanimously. "The American press, particularly those big magazines you work for, is always talking about what's going on in Ghana. Tell you what I'll do: I have a chartered plane out there on the airfield. I chartered an entire airplane to bring my delegates to this conference. You can have a free seat on that plane back to Ghana on Sunday morning. I'll take you there as a guest of the government. You can go where you want to and talk with anybody you choose. Come on and see for yourself what we are doing. Only this one thing," he cautioned, "if you write anything we don't like while you are in Ghana we will put you in jail!"

I was saved from further attack by Madame Ribeiro, the hostess, who took me by the hand and walked toward the dance floor. A stately and gorgeous African, Madame Ribeiro flashed a warm smile as we waited for the music to begin. Then, on the downbeat, Madame Ribeiro began to glide: her flowing back and white flecked gown, made of cloth bearing life-size profiles of Prime Minister Kwame Nkrumah, dissolved into a kaleidoscope as the multicolored lights played upon us. The Addis conference was a revealing thing, at work and at play, by day and by night.

Ethiopia was a significant setting for such a conference. Ethiopia, like Liberia, is a weak argument for independence. Its streets are unpaved, its buildings shabby and crumbling. Even the Ethiopians admit that what few modern conveniences their country now affords were instituted during the period of Italian occupation. Individual rights and freedoms as we know them are almost nonexistent. This state of affairs in Ethiopia and Liberia has long been a thorn in the nationalists' side and the pain was not lessened by Liberian Ambassador John King's remark that his country should not be compared to Ghana because, as he puts it, "We have not had the advantages of colonialism." Even so, the Ethiopians are fiercely proud of their centuries of independence. Heretofore they had not considered themselves Africans, or members of the black brotherhood. When I was a Washington, D.C., newspaperman in the early forties, I was barred from a press conference at the Ethiopian Embassy because I was a Negro.

Even now a residue of this anti-Negro attitude remains in Ethiopia. A Negro secretary at the American Embassy has applied for a transfer after being pelted with stones and called a "slave" by a group of Addis Ababa teen-agers. Several American Point Four officers told me that their Ethiopian house servants frequently refer to American Negroes as "niggers and slaves."

Tucked away high in the mountains, gazing down on the Red Sea and the Gulf of Aden, and with the "wind of change" blowing all about them, Ethiopians, from the peasants to the Palace Corps, realize something new and revolutionary is stirring in their midst. With His Imperial Majesty Haile Selassie himself leading the parade and barking the orders, Ethiopia has done an about-face. Not only does she greet the burgeoning African independent states as brothers, but she has forsaken her long-standing pro-Western stance in favor of the nonalignment gospel that now sweeps all Africa.

"We must keep ourselves free from the political power forces now troubling the world," Selassie told the delegates. "And we must make certain that we do not exchange one kind of colonialism for another." As the applauding delegates well knew, Selassie had first struck out at political colonialism and then attacked economic colonialism, the new whipping boy of the African nationalists.

The man on the street in Addis moves in cadence to the new tune. To be sure, the masses don't know what it is all about; many of the elite who do know what it is all about are disturbed by it. But, like their Emperor, they are forced to admit that African nationalism has struck Ethiopia and that things will never be the same again.

I cannot quote the Ethiopians who talked frankly to me

about their country, for theirs is a strange and fear-ridden land. As in the Dominican Republic, scores of people "get lost" in Ethiopia each year. They simply vanish from the face of the earth. These disappearances are followed by rumors that an antigovernment plot has been nipped in the bud. The mail is censored; telephones, such as there are, are tapped; every social gathering is laced with government spies.

Within the Ethiopian elite, however, there is a hard core of dissidents who feel that their greatest contribution to African nationalism will be to rid Ethiopia of dictatorship, to explode the widely held myth that Ethiopians are a superior people, to rob the Coptic Church of its stifling control over the minds of the masses and of its incredible land holdings.

For Americans, Ethiopia is stark evidence of how much we have lost in Africa, a promise of how much we are yet to lose. For years the Ethiopian economy has been bolstered up by American aid. The country has been peppered by American missionaries. Yet American Embassy and Point Four personnel are bitterly disliked; some of them have been openly assaulted on the streets.

Symbolically enough, we are still trying; our efforts are still being met with contempt. I spent an afternoon with an American Point Four officer who told me of his ordeal with the Ethiopian Minister of Information. Under the strict letter of the law, foreign governments are required to request specific Point Four aid. As in the case with almost all the governments in underdeveloped countries, the Ethiopians themselves don't know what specific programs to request. In this instance, the American spent several weeks working with the Ministry of Information, showing them what they needed to increase the effectiveness of their radio station.

After weeks of cajoling, the American was able to persuade the Ministry to request the needed aid. Then the request was sent off to Washington, where it was approved. Like all Point Four aid, the authorization carried a clause stipulating that the requesting government must accept and sign the authorization within sixty days or the money would revert back to Congress. The American cooled his heels while the authorized program, involving about $150,000, gathered dust at the Ministry. A few hours before the deadline, the Minister of Information signed the agreement.

Incidents such as this (there are scores of them) have cast a feeling of gloom and defeat over most American officials in Ethiopia. And as they sit wondering where and why they failed, Russian technicians are pouring into Ethiopia by the hundreds on the wake of a one-hundred-million-dollar credit the Soviets have given Ethiopia. The Ethiopian Communist party has come back from the dead. The Russians are beginning to operate.

I left Ethiopia convinced that I had just spent two weeks inside a time bomb—a land soon to be rocked by revolution. The world will recoil in shock as masters of the plot unveil irrefutable evidence of medieval torture, replete with dungeons and hundreds of political murders. Unless all the evidence I saw was misleading, the Russians and the African nationalists will emerge as champions of the "liberated Ethiopian masses." The "line" will be that another Western-supported tyrant has hit the dust.

British East Africa consists of four countries: Tanganyika—a United Nations trust territory assigned to Great Britain; Zanzibar—a British protectorate under the direct rule of an

Arab sultan; Uganda—a British protectorate whose future is all but decided; and Kenya—land of the Mau Mau and a continuing headache for the British Colonial Office.

There are less than ten thousand white people in Uganda—a mere drop in the bucket when viewed alongside ten million African Ugandians. Africans have had a majority in the Uganda Parliament and are pressing for independence in 1961. The indepedence move would almost certainly succeed but for "King Freddie," the Cambridge-educated ruler who reigns over the rich central province of Buganda and refuses to go along with either the Africans or the British. Steeped in feudalism, Freddie and his courtiers are unwilling to subordinate Buganda's interests to those of Uganda proper. They boycotted the 1958 elections which gave Africans a parliamentary majority and only stern British opposition has prevented Freddie from forming a separate state over which he, as Mutesa II, would be absolute dictator. African politicians in Uganda are having more trouble with Freddie than they are with the British. If they can quiet him down by early 1961, the chances are that Uganda will be free by the end of the year. Realizing their numerical weakness, settlers have all but withdrawn from Uganda politics and are reconciled to the fact that all of their special privileges will disappear once independence comes.

Zanzibar, that almost mythical island ruled by a sultan and a British governor, is playing little, if any, part in the current African unrest. Arab influence has given General Nasser a strong foothold in Zanzibar, but so far Nasser has been unable to translate this power into an effective campaign on the mainland of East Africa.

The fate of the white man in East Africa, I suspect, will be settled in Kenya and Tanganyika. The Tanganyika verdict will come first because its independence drive is in a more advanced stage than that of the Africans in Kenya. However, I do not think the Tanganyika experience will be controlling. I say this principally because the situation in Tanganyika is greatly misunderstood by non-Africans: this is largely due to confusion over the meaning of the term "multiracialism." The American tendency is to equate multiracialism with integration. In the African frame of reference, multiracialism is quite the opposite. Multiracialism in African politics means the acceptance of the thesis that every racial group should have representatives in the national legislature. If multiracialism were adopted in New York, for example, we would have a Negro member of the legislature representing the Negroes of New York; a Jewish member would represent the Jews; a white Protestant member would represent the white Protestants of New York, and so on ad infinitum. This is precisely what happens in East Africa. There are representatives of the African, European and Asian communities of the same geographic area.

The tendency has been to keep the number of African members to a minimum. Thus, the European and Indian members could always form a majority bloc. Most African politicians tremble at the mere mention of multiracialism and are sworn to abolish it. But Julius Nyerere, the African leader in Tanganyika, embraced multiracialism and taught the Indians and Europeans a political lesson they will never forget.

But before one can understand Nyerere he must first understand Tanganyika.

During the scramble for Africa during the 1880's the Germans grabbed off Tanganyika. When the Germans bit the dust in 1918, Tanganyika was turned over to the League of Nations. The League, in turn, farmed out the responsibility for Tanganyika to Great Britain.

On January 17, 1946, Ernest Bevin, then British Foreign Secretary, announced that Tanganyika would be turned over to the United Nations Trusteeship Council. For fifteen years since then, Tanganyika has been under the watchful eye of the polyethnic United Nations and aggrieved Africans have had a receptive jury listening to their complaints. This, coupled with the fact that there are only 125,000 non-Africans as compared to nine million Africans in Tanganyika, brought on an era of good feeling that made the moves of Julius Nyerere possible. Another factor in the Tanganyika experience is the co-operative movement. Since 1922 Africans and white settlers have been working together in co-operatives designed to increase cash crops and to bring higher prices for these crops. The Africans participated as landowners and as equals. Thus a reservoir of good will, so badly missing in most of Africa, was built up between African and settler farmers.

It was against this background that Julius Nyerere, a former schoolteacher, organized TANU (Tanganyika African National Union) in 1954. Even so, TANU was vigorously opposed by the British government. Several branches of TANU were refused registration in 1956, '57 and '58; four branches were declared unlawful in 1957. As a result, it was not until late 1958 that TANU was able to show its real strength. Nyerere accepted the settler demand for multiracialism but, in return, insisted that each voter have three votes. This gave every voter the right to vote for all three—African, European and Indian—members from his community. The non-Africans felt sure they had the better of it since the constitution called for the election of ten Africans, ten Indians and ten Europeans. What they didn't expect was that a group of liberal Europeans and Indians would announce for the legislature in opposition to the candidates put up by the regular settler and Indian organizations. Under Nyerere's guidance, the Africans swamped the polls, put their own ten men in office and then voted in the liberal Indians and Europeans who supported all-out African government. This made it possible for Nyerere to organize the government, and during the two years of this legislature Tanganyika has moved to the brink of independence.

Nyerere is so certain of his status that, during the Conference of Independent African States, he offered to delay independence for Tanganyika until Kenya and Uganda were ready to combine with him. The move fell on deaf ears—for reasons that will soon become apparent—but it was an indication of the man that is Julius Nyerere.

In 1960, Tanganyika held new elections under a new constitution which outlawed the three-vote parity clause. But Nyerere couldn't care less. The same constitution calls for fifty African members of Parliament as opposed to ten Indians and ten Europeans.

I met Julius Nyerere briefly during the Addis conference. My own feeling is that he is the wisest and most soberminded African politician of them all. I would say nothing to dim his luster. Yet even Nyerere is steeped in African nationalism. During several appearances before the United Nations in New York, Nyerere made it clear that Africans, as indigenous people, should run their own governments. His political party, TANU, does not accept non-Africans as members. However, I have been told recently that this racial ban will be rescinded.

Nevertheless, there is more racial good will in Tanganyika than there is in all the rest of Africa put together. That even Nyerere must ban non-Africans from his political party is a disturbing comment on the state of race relations in Africa. No one who knows Julius Nyerere believes he personally is antiwhite. He most certainly is not, and I am certain that his is the loudest lamentation over the state of affairs. Yet no one who knows Africa would suggest that Nyerere, or any other African politician for that matter, could weld his people together in any other way. At least Nyerere has a group of white liberals who support him and whom he supports. This is a major step forward; whereas in Kenya, to Nyerere's north, the African politicians don't even pretend any longer. The cry for the white men to get out of politics can be heard the length and breadth of Kenya. And the loudest voice for African dominance is from the cosmopolite mouth of Tom Mboya.

There was a gentle but firm knock on my door. It was only eight o'clock in the evening but I was already in bed. My first day in Kenya had been something of a strain. It was hot; I wandered about trying to get a feel of the place. After eight hours of "feeling" Nairobi I was exhausted.

"Who is it?" I asked.

"The porter, Sar."

"What do you want?"

"A visitor, Sar. In the lobby, Sar."

I put on my bathrobe and opened the door. There stood an African, jet black, dressed impeccably in a starched white shirt, black bow tie, a white formal split-tail coat, white pants, a stiff red hat with a black tassel, and no shoes.

"You have a caller, Sar. In the lobby, Sar."

The African bowed and walked away.

I dressed and took the elevator down to the lobby. As I stepped off the elevator I was greeted by a smiling, middle-class African. I knew he was middle-class because he wore a frayed white shirt. He bowed and handed me a note.

"Dear brother Lomax," the note began, "I am sorry I cannot be here to show you about on your first night in Kenya. I must go and stand trial tomorrow in Mombasa. It seems that the government thinks I made a seditious speech there. I have asked brother Ocheche, the bearer of this note, and his wife to take you to their home for a real African dinner."

The note was signed by one of Tom Mboya's aides, a man who met me at the airport when I landed in Nairobi and who had pledged to show me how the Africans live in Kenya.

I bowed to Mr. Ocheche. He bowed back. Then we shook hands. By now I had learned the cardinal fact about social life in Africa. Africans are very poor, they are sensitive and embarrassed about this and they contrive all kinds of pageantry to conceal this fact.

"I have called you a taxi," Mr. Ocheche said, "and told him how to get to our home."

It turned out that Mr. Ocheche was traveling on a motor scooter and he wanted his guest to ride in luxury.

The taxi twisted and turned and finally made its way into the maze of an African location. We were lost for several minutes, then the driver isolated the Ocheche home. The African location reminded me of a housing project at dusk. In a sense that is precisely what it was. The Ocheches lived in this monotonous brick barracks because there was nowhere else for them to live.

"You the American?" Mrs. Ocheche cried out as I made my way around to the back of the project, the only entrance to their home.

"Yes. I'm Lomax."

"Welcome," she said, walking out into the semi-night to shake my hand.

We had arrived ahead of Mr. Ocheche. Mrs. Ocheche led me into their home.

"Do not be ashamed to look at our home," Grace Ocheche said. "We want you to see. You are our lost brother, one who was stolen from us many years ago. We want you to see how we live, to go back and tell the world why we are ready to die."

Theoretically an African can live anywhere he chooses in Kenya. As a practical matter he cannot. With the exception of those who are government ministers, all Africans live on locations. The Ocheches lived in one of the better locations, a development built by the city of Nairobi and set aside as an "African dwelling."

The Ocheche home was on the bottom floor of the two-story development. It was little more than a square concrete area partitioned into four rooms. The Ocheches' bedroom, a small bed and a table, was in one section. The dining room, four chairs and a table, was just beyond it. To the left of the dining room there was the kitchen, a wood stove and a few bins for food. Then there was the "second" bedroom, a small area occupied by the Ocheches' infant child and his "day nurse."

There are no lights in the Ocheche home; the toilet, located several yards down the walk from the entrance to the home, is a concrete stall with a suggestively shaped hole carved in the floor.

The word had spread through the location that the Oche-ches were having an American African to dinner. Five men of the community had come over to greet me. They stood and bowed as I walked into the home. They were young men, now that I remember them, but their faces were cold and hard, their fingers gnarled.

"We have heard about the Africans in America," one of them said to me. "But you are the first one we have ever seen." Then he placed his arm across mine. In the light of the dim kerosene lamp, he matched our colors. Then his face broke into a big smile.

"We are brothers," he confirmed. "Welcome home."

"He's been away a long time," Grace said jokingly. "We must make him remember."

Then they began to tell me about how it is to be black in Kenya. What it is like to have just enough education to make you ambitious, how it feels not to be able to realize that ambition. How one feels when he embraces his wife in intimacy, praying all the while that moment will not result in yet another black child who must attend segregated and inferior schools in a land founded by his ancestors yet dominated by strangers.

"I was the first African secretary hired by the white firm for which I once worked," Grace explained. "They had European and Indian secretaries doing the same work I was doing. I earned half as much as the Indians. The Indians earned a fourth less than the Europeans. Yet we all did the same thing. I got an appointment to see Tom Mboya and asked him to do something about it. He looked at my background and hired me as his secretary."

We all stood as her husband, James, joined us. As the conversation developed, I discovered that James is the first, and only, African clerk to be hired by the white firm for which he works. As was true for his wife, James, too, is on a "sliding" wage scale; he earns half as much as the Indians, who earn a fourth less than the Europeans doing the same kind of work, for the same firm.

"And now you see how we live," James said. "All I ask for is the chance to make a decent living and to provide a home for my wife and child. We don't live here by choice. We can't help ourselves."

Then the other African men told me their stories. They all spoke broken English. It was the same talk over and over again; menial jobs and low salaries; inferior education for their children; apartments without heat; homes without lights. All black men went outdoors to the bathroom.

Then, almost as if by signal, all the visitors stood up. They bowed and left the house. I was completely puzzled by this until I realized that Grace was putting dinner on the table. A middle-class African can feed only so many mouths. This would have been an awkward moment in New York's Harlem. In an African location in Nairobi it was all a part of being brothers and neighbors.

After dinner the men came back. We talked about God and man and human suffering.

James and Grace were educated by Christian missionaries. They still go to church but they are no longer Christians.

"I don't know how to put how we feel," Grace said. "We believe in Jesus . . . but I don't know how to put it."

"What she means," James interrupted, "is that we don't know what to believe. In mission school we Africans were taught that we were the sons of Ham; that there was a curse upon us because Ham laughed at his father's nakedness. The mission teachers told us because of this we were inferior; that we must serve the white men all our lives."

The Ocheches did not have a telephone. Even if they had, there were no taxis on the African location. James went out into the night and found a neighbor with a car who was willing to drive me back into Nairobi.

The streets were flooded with lights and laughter. The theater crowd was on its way home. The "members only" sign on the marquee was hardly visible. As we pulled up to the entrance of my hotel a feeling of guilt engulfed me: my room rent per day was more shillings than the Africans earned a week. I fumbled in my pocket for money. The African and I knew the moment for what it was. Then, in a clipped British accent, he solved my dilemma:

"Just give me enough for petrol."

The plight of the rural African in Kenya is even more disturbing. The bone of contention is the "White Highlands," a magnificent and fertile thirteen-thousand-square-mile stretch of land set aside exclusively for white settlers. The settlers hold this land on ninety-nine-year leases, freeholds; Africans are not only forbidden to own land in the area but are not allowed to manage or sublet strips of land from the white settlers. Of the sixty thousand settlers in Kenya only ten thousand live in the "White Highlands." Much of the highlands is undeveloped; mile after mile of rich, untended, but fenced-in land. This must be contrasted with the approximately six million Africans who live on reserves or land units, commonly called "Crown Land." This means that the Africans can be moved from one place to another without notice or consent.

The controversy over the White Highlands began during the first five years of this century when Sir Charles Eliot, then British Commissioner in East Africa, declared that the interior of Kenya must be deemed "white man's" country. Eliot blandly stated that it would be hypocritical not to hold that white settlers' interests were paramount to those of the indigenous people. By appropriating the highlands, the white settlers drove the Kikuyu, the largest and most ambitious of the Kenya tribes, from their traditional farming and grazing land. The Kikuyu until this day claim they were swindled out of the highlands but they have no avenue of redress since they were denied all participation in politics. The proud Kikuyu refused to work the white man's farms and in 1911-12 a British Commission was appointed to probe the shortage of labor on European farms. The principal witness at the hearing was one Lord Delamere, a European settler spokesman and himself the holder of some 150,000 acres of White Highlands. Lord Delamere told the Commission that there was a labor shortage because Africans had their own land and had no reason to work the Europeans' farms. He proposed a disarmingly simple solution: that African land units be curtailed to the point that Africans would have to work European farms in order to live. Lord Delamere carried the day and the 1952 Mau Mau nightmare was the inevitable result.

The very phrase "Mau Mau" strikes terror in the hearts of non-Africans; it calls up visions of enraged Africans romping through moonlit nights emitting curdling cries of vengeance and wielding meat axes soiled by human blood. To the Africans, however—particularly those in Kenya—Mau Mau is the revolt that failed. "Look at it this way," one prominent Kenyan told me. "If the Mau Mau had succeeded in driving the white man out of Kenya, it would have been the greatest revolution in African history. Mau Mau's only sin was failure. It was a revolution against social evils. It failed because not enough Africans participated." I didn't ask him if he had participated. One doesn't ask a black Kenyan that question.

A similar cloud hovers around the person and legend of Jomo Kenyatta, the Oxford-educated Kikuyu tribesman whom the British imprisoned for his alleged role in the Mau Mau blood bath. For the non-African, Kenyatta is the narcotic-crazed, syphilitic, mad African who whipped tribal savagery to a white heat and then unleashed it against the Europeans. For the African, Kenyatta is the only man who had the guts to resort to violence when the white man's laws had blocked all other avenues of redress. Now Mau Mau is dead; Jomo Kenyatta is in jail. But Mau Mau lives and Kenyatta is the undisputed leader of the Africans in Kenya. Mau Mau lives, though dead, because in the wake of its bloodletting the British lapsed into unprecedented freneticism—freneticism that led to change; change that made life better, at least a little bit so, for the Africans. As a result, Mau Mau gets the praise now that Africans can enter hotels, cafés and most of the theaters of Kenya without fear of discrimination or insult. They can enter, that is, if they can get the money to pay their way. And Kenyatta leads, though shackled, because the British have not only allowed him to become a martyr but have compounded the mystique by refusing to free him although he has served his jail sentence. Under the law, the Governor of Kenya reserves the right to keep any African under house arrest after the African has served a jail term if the Governor feels the African is dangerous to the national security. The Governor's ruling on this matter is irrevocable. It cannot be set aside by any court. Kenyatta completed his sentence in the spring of 1960, but the Governor placed him under house arrest in a remote section of the Northern Province. This act offended the sensitivities of educated Africans but it gives Kenyatta a charismatic quality as far as the masses of Africans are concerned.

The mass adulation of Kenyatta is a thorn in the sides of African politicians. Several of them confided to me that they feel Kenyatta has had his day, that he should withdraw from public life and let younger, less tainted hands guide the Africans' future. But, as a public matter, every African politician makes a show of being loyal and true to the Kenyatta legend.

Despite recent changes, the government's control over the freedoms and lives of Africans in Kenya is all but beyond the scope of democratic imagination. Up until March, 1960, Africans were forbidden to have a national political party; their political activity was restricted to districts. The government claimed such restrictions were in the interest of national security. The net effect, however, was hopelessly to divide African leadership and rob the independence movement of central guidance. Now that the restrictions have been lifted, the Africans still must obtain permission from the government-appointed District Commissioner before they can have a mass meeting; they must list the names of those scheduled to speak and give some indication as to just what will be said.

And this is the very thing that keeps Africa in pain; the colonial powers, particularly the British, who are such champions of individual rights and freedoms at home, completely reverse themselves in their colonies. Her Majesty's governors and armed police think nothing of breaking into an African's home, arresting him without a warrant and jailing him without charges. Until recently, Africans were not allowed to grow any export cash crops. Even now their crops are limited by law and they must get government approval before enlarging their plantations. Until recently, they were denied credit facilities. Now credit is available *if* the African can secure the loan with a land mortgage; this, when they are denied the right to own land.

Violations of the right of free speech are even more appalling. I found it almost impossible to believe that soapbox-infested London and tightly censored Nairobi are under the same government. This is why only the extreme voices are heard in Africa today. There is no middle ground, no room for the well-educated voice of reason. The white man in Africa made an unforgivable mistake when he turned his back on democracy. And Kenya is a prime evidence of that error. One day soon there will be trouble in Kenya—trouble that could have been avoided if the white Kenyans had followed the most elementary forms of civilized behavior. And when the trouble comes the world will have forgotten—or will proceed immediately to forget—all I saw and reported here. The charge will be that the Africans are a wild and bloodthirsty bunch. This "line" will allow the white world to comfort itself, feel certain that it is and always has been on the side of the angels. The Africans, if I have understood them correctly, will not even stop to argue back.

C. B. Madan, the forty-three-year-old member of Legeco—as the Kenyans call their Parliament—from the Indian community, was born in Kenya. His family has lived in Kenya for almost a hundred years. Like most Indians, Mr. Madan's ancestors came to Kenya as indentured servants to work on the Uganda railroad. The early Indians were technicians and artisans and their 125,000 offspring now form Kenya's merchant and artisan class; they are the clerks, the technicians, the shop foremen; they run the banks, stores and pawnshops.

"There is nothing to talk about any more," Mr. Madan said to me frankly. "There is going to be an African majority in Parliament and independence is coming. There will be changes and the Indian people must face up to it. We may as well make up our minds to work with an African government. We cannot sit on the fence."

For several years the Kenya Indian Congress advocated self-government within the British Commonwealth. What the Indians sought was a continuation of the present system in which each racial community is assured of a certain number of seats in Parliament. The Africans, of course, reject this proposal. They insist that every member of Parliament should be elected from a common roll without concern for race, color or creed. In practical terms this means that Kenya would have an all-black Parliament, for Africans are in the majority in every community and will most certainly vote along racial lines (even in the White Highlands the African "squatters" outnumber the white settlers).

The Lancaster House agreement, which assured an African majority in the coming elections, all but sealed the death warrant for Indian politicians. Probably in the coming election—certainly in the one to follow—all Indians will be removed from office.

But beneath the politics of it, there is simmering hatred and bitterness in African-Indian relationships. The Africans accuse the Indians of being part and parcel of the oppression they have known so long. Like the Harlem Negro who turns against the Jews because the Jews are the symbols of all the bills that cannot be paid, the Africans look upon Indians as "economic bloodsuckers," a people not really interested in the life of the country.

Even Indian leaders are hard pressed to defend themselves against this charge in the wake of the mass exodus of Indians out of Kenya now that an African Parliamentary majority is a certainty. One travel agent in Nairobi told me that every available space on ships and planes into India has been booked for the next several months. An Indian leader estimated that Indians have sent upwards of twenty million pounds out of the country since the Lancaster House agreement was reached.

"That money will never be put to work in Kenya again," he said. "It's salted away in European banks."

But the bulk of the Indians, civil servants and clerks, are stuck in Kenya. This is all the home they have. There is nowhere for them to run. They sit there—behind bank rails, post office windows, store counters, showcases—waiting, while well-scrubbed, barefoot African janitors peep over their shoulders.

"I am surprised that you wanted to see me," Air Commodore E. L. Howard-Williams said as we walked toward the lounge of my hotel. "Most reporters who come to Kenya talk to the Africans and think they have all there is to the story. They don't care a farthing about what we white settlers have to say."

Mr. Howard-Williams had quite a bit to say:

"I think Kenya should be independent. I think the Africans must one day run the country. But first I think the British government should give us ten million pounds to launch a full-scale education program for these Africans. That will take from ten to twenty years. That's the only way to do it. I've said this on the floor of Parliament and I've told it to the Colonial Secretary.

"Now, I realize I'll get nowhere with this," Mr. Howard-Williams admitted. "So I have asked Mr. Mboya and his African friends to give us Europeans the following assurances: a promise that land and other properties will not be confiscated once Africans are in control, and a promise that we will be free to send our children to schools of our own choice. And I have asked the British government to impound certain Kenya money to guarantee that the Africans will respect and honor such an agreement once it is made.

"The Africans can't run this country. Only the Europeans can run it and we are not going to stay here if it means our children will have to go to school with Africans. The standards will be lowered at the schools and we will not accept that. The blacks can head the government but they don't have the brains and talent to run the country. I have told them Europeans will stay if the Africans are willing to pay the Europeans extra money to provide all-white, European schooling for their children.

"Now, I blame the American government for all this trouble we are having in Africa," Howard-Williams concluded. "You people have been hounding away at this freedom and independence thing and you have turned all the white people in Africa against you. You don't practice it at home yourselves. Why do you want to force it down the throat of the white man in Africa? America is going to have to bear the blame for whatever happens in Africa."

As I listened to Mr. Howard-Williams I realized how unrepresentative he was of the white people I had met along the streets, in the hotels and airlines offices of Nairobi. Men like Howard-Williams do not speak for the younger generation of white people, who view Kenya as their home and are quite willing to live there under African rule provided they can be given basic protections. Nobody speaks for these white Kenyans. Only the extreme voices can be heard amid the tension.

Panicked whites are leaving Kenya in droves. Mr. Howard-Williams estimated to me that almost a fourth of the country's wealth had been shipped out into foreign banks.

The Kenya newspapers carry argumentative editorials saying, "Freedom and independence must be prepared for. That will take years." But the same editions carry half-page ads from a Johannesburg realty firm saying, "The future will be brighter, the future will be whiter in sunny South Africa—the only large white community in Africa."

I asked Howard-Williams if he planned to stay in Kenya once Africans came to power. He looked at me over the top of his glasses. Then he smiled. "You're damn right I'm going to stay. Somehow the Africans and I are going to make out."

"Tell you a story," he said just before we parted. "During the Lancaster House conference I sat across the table from Tom Mboya. Every day when I took my seat I placed a small Union Jack [the British flag] on the table in front of me. One day the flag fell down. I didn't realize it until Mboya handed me a note: 'Have you capitulated?' I wrote him back: 'To you, yes; to your politics, never!' "

Shortly after I arrived in Kenya the local papers began carrying stories to the effect that members of the Kikuyu tribe were reviving oath-taking. According to the press reports the Kikuyu were taking oaths similar to those administered by the Mau Mau. A few days later, the government information officer called me at my hotel and invited me to attend a press conference at the Central Government Building on the following morning.

I had a pretty good idea what the press conference would be about. The Kenya Minister of Defense had held a hush-hush meeting with several African leaders the night before and told them that the Governor was about to take action against the oath-takers. The entire discussion was "leaked" to me within an hour after the meeting had adjourned.

Consequently I arrived at the Central Government Building ready and willing to ask nasty questions. I had talked the matter over with several newsmen based in Kenya; they too wanted to ask nasty questions. But they had to stay in Kenya; I didn't and it was agreed that I would play the role of devil's advocate.

As I made my way down the long third-floor corridor leading to the conference room, my eyes fell upon the sign on a washroom door. I stopped, frozen in my tracks.

"Men: European," the sign said. I couldn't believe it, yet there it was. I walked a couple of doors down the hall and there was another washroom door—"Men: Asian." Summoning a full head of steam I raced up and down the corridor looking for a door marked "Men: African." There was no such thing.

That did it.

"My God," I said to myself, "Africans can't even go to the toilet!"

I decided that I would ask an explanation for this state of affairs in the middle of the press conference. Segregated washrooms were bad enough but for the Africans not to have a washroom at all was much too much!

I cornered Douglas Willis, the BBC Kenya correspondent whom I had met in Ethiopia and trusted, and told him what I planned to do. Doug broke into laughter. I had stumbled over one of the elementary facts of multicultural life. "European" toilets, it turned out, have seats, whereas "Asian" toilets are nothing more than a hole carved in the floor. As to the facilitation of one's needs, any man—be he African, Asian or European—could use either toilet, depending, of course, on whether he was in the mood to sit or squat!

Chief Colonial Secretary Mr. W. F. Coutts walked into the press conference flanked by Mr. Henry Swann, the Minister of Defense, and two African government Ministers, Ronald Ngala and Dr. J. G. Kiano.

In a terse announcement, Mr. Coutts said that government security forces had just completed a surprise roundup of Africans suspected of giving or receiving oaths. The government records showed that there had been eleven oath-taking ceremonies in the past two months, Mr. Coutts said. Approximately one hundred Africans had been arrested during the midnight operation and they were to be sent off to a detention camp at Lamu, deep in the heart of the Central Province.

These Africans had been arrested without warrants, detained without trials. However, the government had set up a tribunal to which the detainees could address requests to have their cases reviewed.

"We all fear anything like the return of the national emergency," Mr. Coutts said. "And we hope that kind of action will not be necessary."

Then, in the next breath, Mr. Coutts announced that there would be a ban on "subversive" secret societies. Some of the oath-givers had collected money which was sent to yet undisclosed sources, Mr. Coutts told us. As a result the government was announcing a ban on all fund-raising by Africans. Until further notice no African can collect money for any purpose without a permit from the District Commissioner.

What crimes had these people committed? How had they threatened the security of Kenya?

During the question period Mr. Coutts said the oath-takers had done little more than go through a vulgar ritual during which they swore: (1) to keep silent on oath-taking, (2) not to co-operate with the government or any government officer, (3) to work to rid Kenya of white settlers, and (4) to induce others to take such an oath. Only in one instance, Mr. Coutts said, did an oath contain a "death or violence" clause.

I asked Mr. Coutts if this meant that all secret societies were now banned in Kenya.

"No," he laughed. "Just those that are inimical to the national interest."

"How does one decide which secret society is inimical to the national interest?"

"The Governor alone decides that," Mr. Coutts said.

"Is there any law that spells out the kind of societies to be avoided so a citizen can read it and know what's required of him?"

"No, there is no law. It's up to the Governor."

After the press conference I had lunch with one of the African Ministers. He was embarrassed that an outsider had seen him forced to sit humiliated and tongue-tied while a hundred of his fellow Africans were jailed without charges.

"One day," he said midway through the meal, "you will come back to write about Kenya under black rule. And the first thing you members of the Western press will want to know will be whether we African politicians plan to protect the rights and freedoms of white individuals."

That afternoon, I sat in on a Labour Department Board of Inquiry session. The board was seeking the facts behind a strike by slaughterhouse workers at the Kenya Meat Commission on June 5. The striking workers are members of the Kenya Distributive and Commercial Workers Union, an affiliate of the Kenya Federation of Labor, and were represented at the inquiry by Tom Mboya, Secretary of the Federation.

Mboya submitted affidavits and testimony to show that employees had been subjected to "unnecessary discharge, threats, use of bad language and beatings."

A spokesman for management insisted that these grievances, particularly the beating allegation, had never come to their attention.

Mboya countered by introducing a court record which showed that an employee had died following a beating at the hands of a Kenya Meat Commission officer. The Court had found in favor of the worker's widow and the white officer had been ordered to pay her eight hundred shillings (forty dollars) for the death of her husband.

These are the things that are being remembered by the Africans in Kenya; these are the things every African politician must vow to abolish as he takes to the stump for the coming elections. This is the hour of impatient expectations among the Kenya Africans. To a man, they are convinced that they will have their independence within a year. Every African politician I talked with frankly admitted that they were not "ready" for independence in the current sense of that phrase. They know they don't have clerks, technicians, teachers, anything approaching the reservoir of talent needed to run a modern country.

"The government planned it this way," Taita Towett, the Assistant Minister of Agriculture, told me. "If it was left to them we would never be ready. If we are not ready it is their fault. They denied us every opportunity to get ready. Now we want independence. We'll find people to help us run the government."

Early in February, 1961, the voters of Kenya will go to the polls. When the ballots are counted, the Africans will have a parliamentary majority for the first time in modern history. When Legeco assembles, the British-appointed Governor will ask if the government "have" a majority. If Her Majesty's government lacks a majority the Governor will exercise his right and appoint a sufficient number of members to Parliament to assure the government of a majority. The Governor will never get to use that authority. When the question of a government majority is raised, a designated number of Africans will cross the aisle and take government seats. That will be that. As everybody involved knows, the Africans are not with the government; they will play this game of pretense to keep the Governor from packing Parliament with progovernment people. This done, the Africans will unite and appoint an African as Head of Parliament. When he is elected, and he will be for the Africans have the votes to do it, the first item of business will be a motion to send him off to London to demand immediate independence.

This, in practical terms, is the result of the Lancaster House talks in London between British Colonial Secretary Iain Macleod and Kenya leaders (African and white) earlier this year. The only question still to be settled is whether the African head of Parliament will be youthful Tom Mboya or his arch political foe Ronald Ngala.

If Tom Mboya does not become the first Prime Minister of Kenya it will be because too much adulation abroad created enemies for him in Africa. For several months Mboya was the object of a bitter attack by Kwame Nkrumah and Kenya freedom fighters in Cairo. The Cairo attack was a subtle thing: word was spread that Mboya was "living it up in foreign countries," that he had "sold out to the Jews." (The latter rumor was peppered with libelous charges which even the Cairo Kenyans admitted to me could not be proved.) The Nkrumah attacks were bold and open: Mboya was accused of "drinking champagne from the American slipper." Ghana papers editorialized that Mboya had betrayed the African people.

Then, late this spring, opposition to Mboya inside Kenya crystallized into an organization. Until then, Mboya's Kenya African National Union (KANU) was the only African political organization. Most of the African members of Parliament and all but one of the four African Ministers defected from KANU and formed KADU (Kenya African Democratic Union).

"Even God has an opposition," Assistant Minister of Agriculture Taita Towett said to me. "Why should Mboya run unopposed?"

Ronald Ngala, Minister of Education and Mboya's strongest foe, was more specific.

"I helped Mboya organize KANU," he told me. "When I got back from America in May of this year I realized that Mboya was becoming a dictator. It was clear that he was determined to suppress free speech among the Africans and Europeans. Mboya's boys booed and then stoned Mr. Towett because he said something they didn't like. It also became clear that Mboya was out to form a coalition of the Kikuyu and Luo tribes and dominate all the other tribes in Kenya. Mboya has a land scheme up his sleeve once independence comes and the other tribes fear he plans to short-change them. The Masai particularly are worked up about this."

"Then there is this," Ngala continued. "Mboya is using American aid for political purposes. Admittedly this is private aid but we feel such aid should not be at the disposal of one man. American labor unions gave him the money to build his labor center; now he uses the center as a political headquarters. He uses the unions as the basis of his political organization. He uses the student scholarships granted by private Americans for the same kind of political purposes."

Tom Mboya is not an easy man to know. Many foreign observers characterize him as "vain." I found him fastidious almost to the point of a fault. He is an alert man in his late twenties. There can be no doubt that he has a tendency to take his press notices seriously. I could "feel" Mboya because I know scores of American Negroes who are just like him, and the same reasons account for him and them. Mboya has been cast in the role of the "exceptional" African. He is an African, there can be no doubt of that. His skin is jet black, his hair kinky, almost unkempt, and he smiles at times when you know he is not amused. His eyes are large; they shift almost constantly and you are never quite sure he is really involved with you and what you are saying. Rather one feels that Mboya is involved with himself, how what you are saying or doing involves him. When he does warm up to you, you can't escape the feeling that he is doing you a favor.

For, you see, Tom Mboya moves in high company. When the giants of the world labor movement gather in Brussels, Mboya is there. His personal friends in the United States include some of the wealthiest and most influential people in the nation. Almost all of them are white.

But for all of his cosmopolitan sophistication, Mboya at heart is a Luo tribesman, a holy terror when he takes to the political stump. The West likes to feel that it has a strong ally in Mboya. It does, but the West would do well to remember that Mboya's closest political associate, Mr. Oginga Odinga (a man almost unknown in the West), has even deeper ties in Russia. Odinga's pro-Russianism adds duplicity to the list of charges leveled against Mboya by his African opponents.

I confronted Mboya with all of the charges against him as we drove to a political meeting in the Kaloloni location just outside Nairobi.

Mboya shrugged off allegations of Odinga's Russian affiliations as the work of wicked politicians. Turning to the airlift Mboya said, "I'll admit our standards are not the same as yours. I'll admit that some of the students don't get into the best schools in America. But this is a crash program. Any kind of education is better than no education at all. Ngala didn't tell you the truth about my using the scholarships for patronage purpose," Mboya added. "I give them to the students I think best qualified."

When I asked why students close to his political opponents never get scholarships he broke into laughter.

"These boys are just jealous," he said, ending the matter. "Now that independence is in sight everybody wants to be a leader. In a few minutes, you'll see the people. Then you will know."

As Mboya walked down the aisle, the audience of some eight hundred stood and applauded.

"*Uhuru* [freedom]," Mboya said, forming a "U" with his fingers.

"*Uhuru,*" the people shouted back.

"It's been a long time since I was with you," Mboya began.

"Where you been?" somebody shouted.

"Out fighting for you!" Mboya shot back. The audience roared with laughter.

"Freedom," Mboya exclaimed, now speaking in English.

"Freedom," they answered.

"Independence!"

"Independence!" the crowd answered in cadence.

"Justice!"

"Justice!"

And with each exhortation the shouts and applause grew

until the long hall was one deafening roar.

"The Europeans know they are finished in Kenya," Mboya said in Swahili, once silence returned. "Now all they want to know is if we are going to pay them for their land. The civil servants know they are done here. Now all they want to know is whether we are going to give them a pension. Every day they stop me on the streets and they ask me, 'Mr. Mboya, are you going to take our land? Are we going to be compensated? Are we going to get pensions?'" The crowd loved it.

"I tell them" Mboya said laughing, "don't ask me to pay you. Tell your troubles to Macleod [the British Colonial Secretary]. Let him pay you. As far as we are concerned the Europeans have lived off the fat of our land. They have had their compensation and their pension. They don't have anything coming. I say it now for all times, we are not going to inherit any colonial debts. If Macleod wants these Europeans to be paid, let him pay them!"

Men dressed in shabby clothes, all they had, women with babies strapped to their backs, others with babies nursing at their breasts, leaped to the floor with the shout of deliverance:

"FreeeeeeDoooooooom!"

"Then the Europeans want to know if they can stay on in Kenya. I tell them 'sure,'" Mboya said, almost doubling up with laughter. The audience knew what he meant. "But if they stay they must get out of politics. We are going to have an all-black Parliament, and an all-black government. We are going to divide the land among our people. If the Europeans want to stay they can stay on as squatters. If they want to work they can work for us, and they must work on contract. They will come when we say come and go when we say go."

The Africans applauded and screamed with glee. Tom Mboya was on the stump. He was hustling votes, keynoting a political campaign eight months before the election date. His platform was crystal-clear: he promised to submit the Europeans to every indignity and deprivation they have visited upon the Africans for a century.

Then Mboya said a few words about his African opposition. He called them "quislings," "agents of settlers and imperialist forces," "tribalists who would take us back to the days when tribes fought each other in the streets of Nairobi." Turning specifically to Ngala, Mboya said, "He went off to the United States and came back acting like a pregnant woman. He wanted an office in KANU and he lost. Now he wants to call me a dictator. But when the votes are counted we'll win eight to one in their own tribal districts."

Tom Mboya became reverent. His voice well modulated, his eyes lifted to the ceiling, Mboya asked the people, "What did Jomo Kenyatta teach us?" That's the magic name in Kenya. The name every African politician invokes to sanctify his cause. "Kenyatta came back from Europe and taught us that we must not fight among ourselves. All tribes are equal. We are all one."

A solemn hush enveloped the auditorium. Tom Mboya stood rigid, silent, almost as if possessed. Then his right arm shot up into the air. His fingers, their polished nails glittering in the light, formed the "U."

"*Uhuru*," he roared.

This was the benediction.

As we drove away I asked Mboya if he really meant it. He said he did.

We drove through Nairobi some eight miles to the Bahaji location on the other side of town. The audience was waiting and Mboya said it all over again. There was a slight difference, however. Mboya told the people that he was demanding that the government institute a crash program to train Africans for jobs at every level.

"And if we don't have enough Africans to run the government by the time we get independence," Mboya added, "we'll import our black brothers from America to help us."

This was not said for my benefit. Mboya means it. Efforts in that direction are already under way.

Midafternoon on Friday of that week, Ronald Ngala and I left Nairobi in his small English car for Eldama Ravine, some one hundred and fifty miles away. KADU had choosen this picturesque ravine, deep in the Rift Valley Province, as the site for its first political rally. The rally was scheduled for noon on Saturday but Ngala and his advisers arranged a top-level meeting with tribal leaders of the province for Friday night.

We drove through the White Highlands.

"This is what the trouble is about," Ngala said, pointing out to the fertile land. "It's more land than they can possibly cultivate. They have no intentions of cultivating it. They just don't want Africans to live here."

It was difficult to see the settlers' farmhouses. Most of them were tucked away behind tall trees, down winding driveways far back from the road. Every few miles we came to a group of grass huts tucked on the rough side of the valley.

"Those are African squatters," Ngala explained. "Most of them are Kikuyu. They come here to work as farm hands. They live here at the pleasure of the white settlers. They have no rights or security whatsoever."

Shortly before sunset, Ngala stopped the car and pointed to a sprawling farm. None of the land in sight was under cultivation. "That is the farm of an Englishwoman," he explained. "Her land runs twelve miles in one direction. She is a widow. She lives there alone." Then he lowered his head and drew on his pipe. "Our people need that land."

We arrived at Eldama Ravine shortly after nine o'clock, just as the moon was coming over the top of the far-off mountains. The headquarters for the meeting was in a school building sitting in the midst of a flat stretch of land. We arrived just in time. For shortly after Ngala parked the car tribesmen began to come over the hills, up through the valley, singing songs, dancing and driving cattle before them. They seemed to be coming out of the ground on all sides of the flatland. Once they reached the edge of the schoolyard, they pitched camp and built fires, each group to themselves. Then they butchered the cows and began to roast the meat.

One by one the headmen made their way into the school for the meeting with Ngala and his associates.

For more than one hour I made my way among the tribesmen, sampling meat wherever I roamed. I will never forget how the Kipsigi tribesmen roared with laughter because their American brother couldn't join them in downing a gourdful of hot cow's blood.

When I entered the school I found Ngala and the headmen, some fifty of them, gathered around a blackboard. It took me a few moments to recognize the map drawn on the board. Then I realized that they were dividing up the White Highlands. Speaker after speaker took the floor to stake his tribe's claim to a certain section of the highlands. Occasionally there were conflicting claims but they were readily resolved. Then KADU committed itself to the agreed-upon partitioning of the highlands once independence was achieved.

Shortly after midnight the meeting adjourned. The politicians went out and joined the feast that lasted into the early hours of the morning.

Five thousand cheering Africans poured into the ravine for the rally on Saturday morning. They came by bicycle, truck, motor scooter, automobile and on foot. The morning arrivals were from Eldama Ravine itself but were little, if any, different from the tribesmen who came in from the hills and valleys on Friday night—some of them as far as a hundred miles away.

The colorful Suk tribesmen, some fifty strong, stole the show almost before it began. They arrived on the back of a large truck, their "chignons" and hoop-like ornaments of giraffe hair bobbing crazily in the air. While hundreds of amused Africans gathered about the truck, the Suk freshened their "make-up"—wide swatches of blue and white paint that covered most of their faces—and affixed their nose plates. On signal, the driver lowered the back gate of the truck to form a gangplank and the Suk, in a close-rank formation, marched out onto the flatlands singing a song of welcome. It was a haunting and beautiful tune, rendered in perfect four-part harmonv. As their fellow Africans marched along in cadence the Suk paraded around the meeting ground bursting with song. It had been a long time since I heard a harmony such as this. More than twenty years, in fact: this was the kind of tune, couched in just this close instinctive harmony, that my grandfather's congregation sang just before he rose to preach hell-fire and damnation.

Marching with the Suk I had an anachronistic wish: that these incredibly warm, kind and uncomplicated people could march down the aisle of that south Georgia Negro Baptist church while Grandfather explained the mysteries of the dry bones in the valley.

What a time we would have had! What a time; what a time! But it is too late now. The time is out of joint. The Suk have a faith of their own; even worse, as far as the Suk are concerned, the Christianity grandfather offered is inextricably linked to the fences and laws that keep black men's cattle from grazing in the White Highlands.

With few exceptions, the remainder of the crowd was in Western dress. Every man, of course, carried a cane or stick.

The audience was enthusiastic but, in a very real sense, the rally was anticlimactic. The significant meeting had been held the night before and the headmen had passed the word that KADU and the Kalenjin Alliance (the political organization that binds these peoples) had reached an agreement. Carmine De Sapio never had it so good. Once the headmen gave the word, every vote in the valley would go to candidates sponsored by KADU. There was really nothing to talk about.

Then Ngala, more of a scholar than a politician, and his aides are not quite the spellbinders Mboya is. But in Eldama Ravine they didn't have to be. These tribesmen are the conservatives of Kenya African politics. "Tom Mboya couldn't raise ten votes out here," the British District Commissioner remarked to me. "He's a city boy."

KADU, like KANU, called upon the Europeans and the Indians to get out of politics. The crowd cheered promises of better schools, more land, better housing, higher prices for crops and cattle. Ngala, as did the other eleven speakers, invoked the name of Jomo Kenyatta.

"Once we are in power," Ngala promised, "Kenyatta will be released from house arrest."

"*Uhuru!*" the crowd roared back as a sign of approval.

On the way back to Nairobi, Ngala admitted to me that the coming elections will turn on personalities, not issues. "As of now," Ngala said, "it's a toss-up between KANU and KADU. We must get our city machine going and Tom has to get out in the country. It's too early to say how things will work out. But this we do know," he added, "there will be an African majority in Parliament next year. We will move for immediate independence."

I had been out of touch with the news for thirty hours. As I stood at the desk of the New Stanley Hotel waiting for my key, the headline of the afternoon paper caught my eye.

The Congolese Army had mutinied.

People were tense in Nairobi that Sunday morning. About noon, I felt the whole place was about to snap.

The local radio and the BBC filled the air with Congo horror stories; on-the-spot interviews with hysterical women who had just been repeatedly raped; we heard the wails and cries of children who were lost from their parents. One European businessman came on the air to describe how it felt to squat hiding in the bush while "primeval" black men wrecked his home. He and his family leaped into an aircraft just a few steps ahead of the rampaging "blacks."

The Kenya newspapers shouted, "We told you so!" "It must not happen here!"

By midafternoon, Congo refugees, many of them without funds, all of them frightened and angry, began to flood into Nairobi. "Refugee camps" and "relocation centers" sprang into being as Kenya Europeans raced to the aid of their kith and kin. The white extremists demanded that a white volunteer army march into the Congo.

As I walked through the streets of Nairobi I thanked God it was Sunday. Shops and public offices were closed. There was a minimum of contact between white and black peoples.

Tom Mboya received me in his office at the Solidarity Building. He was dressed in sleek gray Dacron slacks, a yellow pullover coolie jacket with green frog buttons, and black velvet slippers. Mboya was obviously worried.

"Now all hell begins," he said, pounding on the desk. The Congo thing had him by the guts. "This is all we need. . . . Why? Why? Why?"

Mboya's view of the Congo was a good deal different from that of the Kenya Europeans. Mboya was remembering the sordid history of the Congo, the days when Belgians cut out the Congolese's tongues, amputated their arms, enslaved men by the hundreds and raped the Congolese women. Mboya saw naked revenge in the brutal acts against the white men in the Congo; he saw defilement, not lust, in the raping of white women. There was a prophetic note in Mboya's voice as he spoke of Mozambique, Angola and South Africa.

"Africans are still being butchered in these places," Mboya said. "More Congos in the making."

"Even here in Kenya," he added emotionally, "the Europeans don't understand what the Congo means: it means they should give us more freedoms, better treatment. Instead, they see it as reason to curtail what few freedoms we have, as justification for treating us worse."

The following morning I went to the Belgian Consulate in Nairobi to get a Congo visa. The office was jammed with refugees. As I walked into the reception room the women reacted with fright, the men turned a deep red. Three of them moved menacingly toward me.

The receptionist, who had been alerted for my arrival by the American Consulate, explained hastily in French, "He is not Congolese." And once they knew I was an American the tension subsided. The men offered to sell me Congolese francs at reduced rates. They knew, as I did, that the money was absolutely valueless. The women turned warm and friendly. They asked me why the Congolese had turned against them. Here, in these Belgians, was the same tragic incomprehension, total unperceptiveness and nonremembrance of history I had encountered time and time again among white people in the American Deep South. There is, of course, no justification for what happened to these Belgians; but the realization that they did not know *why* it happened taxes the faith of the most devout humanist.

Late that afternoon I left Nairobi for Salisbury, Southern Rhodesia. The Nairobi airport building was overflowing with Congo refugees. One Belgian child, a boy of about three, saw my face and broke into a big smile. He ran from his parents and threw his arms lovingly about my legs, all the while chattering in French. The boy's mother almost fainted; the enraged father snatched the child away and gave me the look of hate. Somewhere deep in the Congo there is a Congolese who looks like me. Once upon a time, he and that little Belgian boy were close friends . . . but now, no more.

We flew almost along the rim of the Katanga Province. Then we landed at Ndola, Northern Rhodesia, a scant one hundred miles from Elisabethville.

All passengers had to disembark while the plane was being refueled.

Weeping women and distraught men were all over the place. Belgian children were dirty, crying and hungry. Their fathers had no money with which to buy food for them. A "hospitality" line was going full blast. Even so, these many people, accustomed to so much luxury and now reduced to so much discomfort and humiliation, were simply not nice for a black man to be near. I avoided crowds; I gave none of them chance to push or shove me.

Two hours later at Lusaka, still in Northern Rhodesia, there was more of the same.

Shortly after two o'clock in the morning, we landed at Salisbury.

I was the first passenger to clear customs and was about to board the airlines bus into town when one of the customs officers pointed to me and demanded, "Who cleared him?"

"I did," the officer to his left replied.

"Bring every one of his damn bags back here!"

The African porter returned my bags to the customs counter and then joined several other porters who were huddling, frightened for me, in a corner.

The officer opened my bags one by one. He shook every garment, then examined it to make sure it had been worn. If not, he could confiscate all my luggage on the grounds that I had "undeclared new goods." He examined all notes, interview after interview.

"So you have been talking with Mboya?" he asked angrily.

I nodded "yes."

Then he turned to my cameras. He took both of them apart and examined them. All of a sudden his eyes danced with glee. I had three rolls of unopened 16 mm. film.

"These are new items," he shouted. "You didn't declare them. I'll have to confiscate all your luggage!"

I recognized all this for what it was. Not one of my fellow passengers' luggage had been opened. They, as indeed I did at first, walked through customs without even being questioned.

I asked for permission to call the American Consulate.

"You sit down and keep your mouth shut," was the tart reply.

The officer grabbed the film, along with all my interview notes, and disappeared into a room at the back of the customs counter. Ten minutes later he emerged crestfallen. He had obviously been overruled by a superior officer.

The episode had taken more than an hour. The bus, loaded with my enraged fellow passengers, was still waiting. For the airlines was committed to drive even me into town.

Later that morning I took a taxi to the home of J. G. Silundika, whom I had met in London with Joshua Nkomo.

Silundika's home was a beehive of activity. Just before my arrival, police had raided the offices of the National Democratic party and all of the party leaders were expecting to be arrested momentarily. The police had found two incriminating bits of evidence: a memorandum containing the phrase "we ex-detainees" and a banner reading "Forward, Ever, Backward, Never!" These items, according to the police, were irrefutable proof that the National Democratic party was, indeed, a front for Nkomo's outlawed African Nationalist Congress. Michael Mawema, the president of the party, was rushing back from Uganda, where he had been holding talks with Hastings Banda.

Mawema, Silundika and their aides went about their planning with astonishing calm for men who knew arrest was imminent. With the casualness of a New England town meeting they laid their plans:

A. Certain specified officers would remain in Salisbury and be arrested.

B. An "underground committee" composed of Africans whom police didn't suspect as being members of the party would create community "reaction." They would see to it that there were mass demonstrations as soon as the arrests occurred.

C. Three men were sent to Bulawayo, some three hundred miles away, to start agitation there.

D. Two men were sent to the Congo. Their assignment was to keep "pipelines" open. In plain language they were to arrange for aid from Patrice Lumumba.

E. One man left Salisbury by night to make his way to Ghana; another was sent to Cairo. Thus the party would have representatives at the two money sources.

F. A coded cable was sent to Nkomo bringing him up to date.

For two days Silundika and his men took me around Salisbury, showing me as much as they could under the circumstances. We were followed day and night by African members of the Central Intelligence Division. These African secret service men are a source of much tension among the African people. In a sense they are doing a job, the only kind of police job they are allowed to do. Even so, they are not allowed to carry arms and are always under the watchful eye of a European superior parked in a car not too far away. But nationalistic Africans do not feel the issue is one of law and order but one of white domination, and look upon these African police as traitors.

They are well-known members of the African community; their names are kept in what one African leader calls a "futures" book. But there is yet another twist to the story of the African policeman: where could one find a more advantageous job for an underground member of the African nationalist movement?

The condition of Africans in the Federation follows the general lines: they live on locations; few of them have jobs above the menial level; they are allowed to own the walls and roofs of their homes but not the ground on which the house sits. If more than eleven of them assemble at one place they must have a permit which states the nature and purpose of the meeting, along with the names of those in attendance.

As I walked out of my hotel on the morning of my second day in Salisbury, I was greeted by an exceptionally friendly African. He grabbed my hand, shook it, said he wanted to be friends with me. While the African was grinning and bowing, a European leaned out the window of a car parked just across from the hotel and took my picture. The secret service boys had seen me with the African politicians. This was their way of getting a file on me.

I noted the license plate of the car and walked away from the African. Later in the day, I discussed the matter with officials at the American Consulate. Their only advice was, "Be careful."

I returned to my hotel that afternoon and discovered that Judge Samuel Pierce, a Negro and a Judge of New York's Court of General Sessions, had just arrived. Judge Pierce was spending several months in Africa seeking out worthy projects for a Midwest foundation interested in granting private aid to Africans. Our paths had crossed briefly in Nairobi, and he and Mrs. Pierce had been subjected to the same tensions I faced. Between trying to get his wife a reservation back to New York before the situation worsened and trying to interview African politicians before they were jailed, Judge Pierce had little time to relax. On my last day in Salisbury, however, the Pierces and I had dinner together in the hotel dining room.

"I saw Mawema's car parked out front a few minutes ago," Judge Pierce said to me. "Were they visiting you?"

"No," I replied.

"Then who were they visiting?"

Before I could answer, Judge Pierce remembered some faces he had seen in the hotel lobby. He adduced what I already knew: the African politicians were closeted with the Chinese Communists.

Even before I left New York, I resolved that I would go inside South Africa. My resolve was motivated by reliable reports that African political activity had gone underground in the wake of Sharpville and was now more virile than before. After several days of delicate negotiations I was introduced to a New York "contact" who, in turn, agreed to put me in touch with the South African underground. We moved on the assumption that the South African government would not grant me a visa. There were three strikes against me: I was an American, a reporter and a Negro. The chances that I would be given a visa were all but nil.

I applied for the visa, however, and presented papers showing that I had an assignment in Basutoland, a British protectorate completely surrounded by South Africa. As every traveler to Basutoland must, I asked for a transit visa that would allow me to cross the Union of South Africa. The visa officer told me flatly that it would take his government several weeks to make a decision on the application and that I would be apprised of the verdict through the South African High Commission in Nairobi.

My chain of contacts had links in London, Cairo, Addis Ababa, Nairobi and Salisbury. Coded letters and cables moved ahead of me; at each point I was met by Africans who gave me only enough information to make the proper contact at the next stop along my route. According to the plan, I would make my way to the border of South Africa, where Africans, dressed as tribesmen, would spirit me through the bush into the country. I was then to be provided with credentials that would allow me to move about. It was a risky plan, for them and for me.

From New York to Cairo the plan went according to schedule. In Addis, however, I found my contacts apprehensive. A few days before I arrived in Ethiopia a well-known South African writer and critic of the government had escaped into

Uganda. He wrote a series of articles describing his escape route and there was a good chance that the South African government was now alerted to some of the contacts I was yet to employ.

After an all-night talk, my Ethiopian contacts and I decided on a new route. This meant I would have to go it alone; the Ethiopians provided me with key names and addresses, but it would be up to me to make new contacts along the way.

I visited the South African High Commission on the morning I arrived in Nairobi. As expected, they had no word on the fate of my visa application. My Kenya contacts had a mixed bag of news for me. They also felt that the regular underground route had been dangerously imperiled by the recent series of articles, but word had come through that I should hasten into South Africa by whatever route possible because a significant story was in the making.

I passed up a chance to go into the Congo and left Nairobi for Salisbury as quickly as my work would allow.

The underground links in Salisbury moved with extreme caution. Under no circumstances could they risk being identified with the African politicians of Southern Rhodesia. These men are South Africans, but they are working in Rhodesia under false papers. They were alarmed when I told them the Rhodesian police were following me and we broke off contact for a day while new means of communications were arranged. We met in a field behind a church on an African location at three o'clock the following morning. Had anyone followed me, my contacts would have seen him long before he saw them: they would not have been there. A new link had been forged in the underground chain; a new contact was waiting for me in Bulawayo. From there I was to be taken by car directly into Johannesburg.

Then the unexpected happened: the South African government granted my application for a visa. The praise or criticism, as the case may be, goes to the American Consulate in Salisbury. I mentioned the South African government's obduracy on this matter to an official of the Consulate when I first arrived in Salisbury. He contacted his counterpart in the South African Consulate and the visa was granted.

My contacts and I were pleased by this turn of events. There was a very close working relationship between the police in South Africa and the police in Southern Rhodesia; this came to the fore just after Sharpville when the Federation refused to allow refugees from South Africa to enter its territory. Those who attempted to enter the Federation were arrested and extradited to South Africa. This attitude on the part of the Southern Rhodesian government caused loud grumbling among Rhodesian Africans. By contrast, the government of Southern Rhodesia hastened to give aid and comfort to white refugees from the Congo. The disparity between the treatment afforded white refugees from the Congo and black refugees from South Africa deepened the Africans' conviction that the Southern Rhodesian government, in fact the entire Federation, supported not only white domination but the killing and jailing of Africans as well.

We knew that I had been followed; we had no way of knowing whether the telephone in my room at the hotel had been tapped. There was a possibility that my mail, both incoming and outgoing, had been read. If either of these possibilities had occurred then the South African government was fully aware of my determination to enter the Union.

For my African friends and me, the issuance of my transit visa was proof positive that the South African government did not know what I was up to.

Our plans had to be overhauled because of the new development. Coded telegrams were sent outlining my new plans to contacts in Bulawayo and Johannesburg. Several hours later word came back giving me the phone number I was to call once I reached Johannesburg.

Late Friday morning, July 16, I left Salisbury for Johannesburg. The flight was uneventful. There was none of the tension I had experienced en route from Nairobi to Salisbury. There were several refugees from the Congo aboard, however, but most of them were American missionaries. I found them, on general balance, calm about what had happened in the Congo and, strangely enough, sanguine about the possibility of an early return to their mission posts.

I did not relax, although I was going into the Union of South Africa legally. As with Mississippi, no sane black man enters South Africa without some reservations. While the plane droned on, I tried to conceive of every possible action the government of South Africa could take once I landed, then I planned a counteraction:

They could assign a security man to travel with me every step of the way. If they did, I would go directly to Basutoland and then work my way back into South Africa illegally.

They could assign a security man to trail me from afar. If they did, it would be up to me to isolate my shadow and dodge him. Under no circumstances would I lead him to my contacts.

A third possibility was that the South African government would simply ignore me. I knew what I was up to but they didn't; chances were they would not make any special efforts to keep track of my movements.

In any event, my basic plan was to get hotel accommodations in Johannesburg and spend a day or so moving about on my own. Only after I was certain that I was not being followed would I contact the South African underground.

The plan seemed simple enough, but I began to knot up on the inside with the announcement that we would soon be landing in Johannesburg. My personal tension was relieved momentarily by a routine event which both amuses and annoys passengers arriving at Jan Smuts Airport for the first time.

After the plane came to a stop in front of the terminal we were instructed to keep our seats until the health officer came on board and sprayed the plane. We had arrived from a critical yellow fever area and it was perfectly understandable that South African health authorities felt the need to disinfect the plane. However, this bit of rationality did not extract the humor from the moment when the health officer walked through the plane spraying passengers and baggage with something that looked like a can of Flit. I was the only nonwhite on board and I suspected that I would be drenched with insecticide. It was a moment of self-pity, and nervous humor contrived to relieve my anxiety about what lay ahead. The health officer squirted by me with no more attention than he paid other passengers.

The customs officer was unexpectedly pleasant. We chatted about life in the United States as he checked my declaration form. He did not open my bags.

"This, Mr. Lomax," he said, handing me a long legal form, "is your permit to be in the Union."

I skipped the fine print and read the significant sections: in essence, this was my "pass," the controversial document every black man must have on his person at all times in South Africa. The key clause in the document said I was in transit to Basutoland and that this pass granted me permission to be in the Union for twenty-four hours.

Twenty-four hours!

The stipulation leaped up from the page and hit me in the face with a thud. The officer recognized my concern. There was a wry smile on his face.

"You have twenty-four hours to get to the Basutoland border," he explained. "There you will surrender this pass. On your way back, customs officers in Basutoland will give you another pass good for twenty-four hours that will permit you to travel back to Johannesburg and take a plane to New York."

In all frankness the stipulation was fair. It was then three o'clock in the afternoon and there were two trains for Basutoland that night: one at seven-thirty, the other at nine. I knew this and was certain that the customs officer knew it also. There was only one thing wrong, of course: I didn't really want to go to Basutoland, and twenty-four hours was hardly enough time for me to accomplish my mission in the Union.

"Suppose for some reason I don't make it to Basutoland within twenty-four hours?" I asked.

"It had better be for a good reason," he replied with a smile. Then he gave me the address and phone number of the immigration office in Johannesburg. "If you are delayed, go to this office and they will decide if there is any reason to extend your permit."

This was an unexpected and disturbing turn of events. What bothered me most about the time stipulation was that it meant I would have to make contact with the underground sooner than I had planned, before I could be certain that I was not followed.

I stood near the airlines bus pondering my next move.

"*Uhuru,* brother."

I looked to my left and a smiling African was approaching me. He was well dressed; too well dressed, in fact. If ever a man was born with a police badge in his hand, this African was.

I nodded slightly in his direction and boarded the bus. I wanted no part of his "*uhuru.*"

"Take the back seat," the driver said curtly. I moved to the long rear seat and placed my cabin baggage on the overhead rack. I looked out of the window and saw the African making his way toward an automobile.

If my guess was right he would be waiting when the bus arrived at the Johannesburg air terminal. He was.

The airlines maintained a hostess service just inside the terminal. As passengers claimed their baggage the hostess assisted them in arranging hotel accommodations or securing a taxi. I was at the end of the line. When it came my turn she simply got up from the desk counter and walked away.

One of the African porters approached me. "Wait out there," he said, pointing toward the sidewalk. He picked up my bags and led the way. I stood on the sidewalk and waited. The African who trailed me from the airport sat patiently in a car across the street. The wait lasted more than half an hour. Only after I was in the cab did I realize that the hostess had called the cab company and said, "There is an African over here waiting for a cab. If you have a driver who doesn't mind hauling Africans, send him over!"

"Several drivers refused to come," the hackman told me.

The driver was a white South African. A middle-aged man who described himself as a "fellow who likes everybody but minds his own business. I don't make or break the laws," he said.

I asked him to take me to a hotel, any hotel—it didn't matter as long as I could get a room.

He drove me to three hotels. None would give me a room. We stopped Africans on the street and asked them where we could find an African hotel. Apparently there's no such thing.

It was then well after five o'clock. I told the driver to take me to the office of *Drum* magazine, an African publication. I was certain that somebody there could direct us to a hotel. The office was closed but one of the writers was working late on a special assignment. With some misgivings at first, he agreed to help me find a place to stay. I dismissed the taxi and brought my bags inside the office. The African policeman was nowhere in sight.

After several futile telephone calls the writer located a man who operates a clandestine roominghouse in one of the African locations near Johannesburg. The man agreed to give me a room for the night. I summoned an "African" cab and sped off toward the boardinghouse just as night and cool winter air were settling over Johannesburg.

After we had driven several blocks I ordered the driver to pull up at a sidewalk telephone booth. I dialed the number that had been rippling through my mind like a troubled stream since I left Salisbury. The phone seemed to ring forever. Then:

"Hello." The voice was cautious.

"Grandmother is fine," I replied.

There was a long pause.

"Is she out of the hospital yet?"

"No," I answered, following the prearranged code. "But she soon will be."

I was directed to proceed to a railroad station, check all my baggage and then take a taxi to a bus stop along the road leading out to an African location.

"Board the first bus leaving that point after seven o'clock," the man said and hung up.

Johannesburg does not have segregated buses. It has two separate bus lines: one for Africans, another for white people. Both buses travel the same route but they stop at different points. I waited until seven o'clock and then joined the queue at the African bus stop. At seven-twelve the bus came. We jogged along for several stops. The Africans were full of happiness and laughter. I understood nothing of what they said, of course, but it was obvious that they were regular passengers going home from work.

Just as the bus was coming to a stop, a woman sitting directly behind me leaned forward and whispered in my ear: "Get off at the next stop. Not this one; the next one . . ."

I got a good look at her as she rushed to get off the bus.

The next stop was several blocks away. I alighted into almost total darkness. As the bus pulled away I fished in my pocket for a cigarette.

"Pass," someone demanded.

A white policeman had come from out of nowhere. I produced my permit and tried to appear calm as he examined it. "This isn't the road to Basutoland," he said.

"I know," I told him. "I'm visiting a friend out this way. I'll be leaving for Basutoland on the nine o'clock train."

He returned my permit and walked away. It would have looked suspicious for me to stand at the bus stop. I reasoned that the underground people were close by and saw what had happened. I lit my cigarette and started walking slowly up the street.

I had walked about a half a block when a small car eased up to the curb beside me. It was an English car with the steering wheel on the right-hand side. I could not see the driver's face but I recognized the woman in the front seat beside him immediately: she was the woman from the bus. The back door opened for a brief moment and then we vanished into the night.

As we pulled away the driver spoke up.

"*Uhuru,* brother." It was the African policeman. A cold chill ran through me. They let me shake for a moment and then they both broke into laughter. He was a policeman; he was also one of the leaders of the underground.

We drove to an African home where several trusted Africans had gathered to give me a full report of events inside South Africa since the Sharpville killings.

One of the men present works as a clerk in a hospital during the day. He spends his nights piecing together a horror story: the disappearance of several thousand African youths since Sharpville. After weeks of taking affidavits under circumstances which laid him open to arrest at any moment, he thinks he has come up with the answer. This, in essence, is the story:

The emergency regulations instituted by the South African government in the wake of the recent uprisings empowered police to arrest Africans deemed to be "loiterers." Several thousand teen-agers (some reports say the number runs as high as thirty thousand) have been arrested under this provision. The largest number of arrests seems to have occurred in Alexandra Township, where youths have great difficulty in getting work permits. Thus the youths are caught in a vise: on one hand government officials refuse to give these youths work permits, an indispensable prerequisite for employment; and on the other hand they are arrested because they don't have work permits.

Even during normal times, more than a thousand Africans are arrested each day for violations of the pass law. Most of these Africans have legitimate passes but through an oversight happen not to have the document on their person at the time of the arrest. (I talked with a man who was in his front yard playing with his dog when a policeman walked up and demanded to see his pass. His pass was in the house, less than thirty yards away. He was arrested for not having the document on his person.) When they appear in court these violators are given fines ranging from fifteen to twenty-five dollars. If they are unable to pay the fine they are given jail terms ranging from five to eight weeks.

This is the normal situation in South Africa. The months since Sharpville have been far from normal and the staggering number of youths arrested as "loiterers" must be added to this routine rate of a thousand pass violators per day.

Where are these youths? What has happened to them? This is the mystery the South African underground set out to solve and expose. This is the story they wanted me to rush in and hear.

According to sworn affidavits, the youths were arrested in droves. Parents were not allowed to visit them in jail; they were not allowed legal representation at whatever hearings were held. As far as my informants knew, the youths were not given hearings at all. Scores of parents have given statements saying that officials refused to tell them where the youths are or what has happened to them. South African newsmen are aware of the story but their hands are tied. On July 10, the *Garden City Post,* an African newspaper, published a four-paragraph account of the arrests that contains this sentence: "Nobody is informed what happens to these youths, and the Prisons Act makes it dangerous for newspapers to make their own investigations."

Despite the difficulties involved, the underground has amassed an impressive array of evidence showing that these youths have been put in peonage under the much exposed South African "farm labor" scheme. Under this scheme, pass violators are "allowed" to work on private farms for a few shillings a day. The farmer becomes their jailer; they are locked up at night, denied all rights and privileges. Reports of beatings and murders on these farms comprise the most shocking volume in current African literature. The system has been exposed time and again, particularly by the Anti-Slavery Society and the International Labor Organization.

This time, however, the South African government may have overstepped itself. The reports indicate that several hundred of the youths involved were nationals from Basutoland, Bechuanaland, Southern Rhodesia and Nyasaland who had come into the Union in search of work. If true, the British government could force the issue into the open and launch an inquiry. Affidavits supporting the summary I have just given have been placed with a distinguished member of the House of Commons, a man who has waged a long-standing fight for African causes. He has promised to raise the question on the floor of Commons.

If the affidavits stand up—and it is difficult to see why people, some of them white South Africans, would risk their freedom by swearing to such statements and then lie in the statements—several of the youths were killed while trying to escape from the farms.

"We have done all we can," the Africans told me. "Only world opinion can force the truth into the open."

The next major concern of the African underground is the Bantu Education Act. Under this piece of legislation all professional schools will be closed to Africans after this year. Any African wishing to study medicine or law will have to leave the country. This seems simple enough until you realize that it is all but impossible for an African to get a passport.

A schoolteacher joined the group to tell me how the Bantu Education Act works at the elementary grade level. What she said, in essence, was this:

The law requires that Africans be taught in their tribal dialects. This means African schools are segregated along tribal lines. But even more disastrous, it means many children get little or no education. First of all, it is extremely difficult to find teachers who can teach in some of the dialects. More, most of the dialects are functional rather than technical modes of speech. "How do you teach a child geography," the woman said, as an example, "when his language does not contain any word that means longitude or latitude? If you teach him the words in English you have violated the law!

"The school officials know this, of course," she continued, "but they don't want African children to have any kind of formal education."

The main course in the African elementary schools is something called "Social Science." The intent of this course is to teach the African child how to be an African; how to apply for a pass, how to go about getting a work permit, the location of the nearest police station; how to get in and out of town, what buses he can ride, where he can sit. Special emphasis is placed on learning menial tasks, particularly the duties of servants, and how to address white people.

And this is the way it was all night long. Members of the South African underground, each a specialist in his own field, pouring out their complaints to a reporter in the hope that he would tell the world and that the world would in turn do something about it.

One of the men present was among those detained for burning his pass. He was imprisoned for three months without an indictment or trial. Five days before I arrived, he had been released along with several hundred other detainees and warned not to talk with reporters or appear at any meetings.

Another of the men present is a sports enthusiast. He works as a porter by day. By night he gathers evidence to show discrimination against Africans in the Olympic tryouts. Many of the complaints now filed against the South African Olympic team are the work of this man.

Then there was the man with one leg. He was there to tell me about Sharpville. He heard the noise and shouting in the street; he ran outdoors to see what it was all about. The next thing he knew he was in the hospital, his leg shot off. He knew nothing of the issues involved; he was not a member of the Pan-African Congress. He is now.

These are brave people. They are doing much more than gathering information against the South African authorities. What they are planning and when it will occur are matters that cannot be discussed, of course. But it is no news to the South African government that when the Africans rise up again they will have help from the outside.

The meeting ended shortly before dawn. I slept for about four hours, then I was awakened by my host.

"You must go now," he said. "They must never trace you to my home."

Following his directions, I walked several blocks through the location to the bus stop. The bus was almost empty—the Africans had long since gone off to work—and I fitfully nodded as we jogged into town.

The clock struck eleven as I was retrieving my bags at the railroad station. I had five hours in which to get out of South Africa. Technically, the permit was good for another thirteen hours—midnight of the expiration date. But I was in no mood to argue technicalities with a South African policeman. I suppose I could have visited the immigration office and asked for an extension. But then I would have been asked where I had been since four o'clock the previous day.

The truth is I was anxious to get out of South Africa as quickly and as quietly as possible.

The Congo situation had burdened all the airlines. Reservations out of Johannesburg were all but impossible to obtain. I knew I would get no consideration whatsoever if I showed my face at an airlines office. The telephone was my only hope. On the third call I got an airline clerk who spoke English with what sounded to me like a European accent.

"The best I can do," she said, "is to put you on a waiting list for a flight into Salisbury this afternoon." I was not listening to *what* she said but to *how* she said it. If she was an alien then the chances were she was not prejudiced and would at least give me a fair shake.

I took a taxi to her office. I saw her eyes narrow as I walked in. As I explained my problem she stared down at the floor. Then she began to dial her phone. It took several phone calls, but when she finished I had a reservation on the afternoon plane to Salisbury.

I checked in at the airline terminal and boarded the bus with the other passengers. I had just taken my seat when the driver yelled to one of the African porters: "Tell that God-damn Bantu to get off that bus!"

The porter—the same fellow who had put my bags on the street the day before—motioned for me to get off.

"Wait here," he said, pointing to a lamppost.

I waited. Twenty minutes after the bus had departed an "African" cab sped up. I was getting the red carpet, the special service reserved for Africans. It was a twenty-mile taxi ride. The airline, of course, paid the fare.

That was late in July, 1960. Since then most of the African politicians whom I met in Salisbury have been jailed, as was expected. As also planned, the men I saw then deploying to various cities organized and executed demonstrations that jerked Southern Rhodesia to the brink of a nationwide race riot.

The formation of an Afro-Asian army under the command of the United Arab Republic has been announced in the public press.

Kenya's Tom Mboya almost lost his life in an automobile accident while en route back to Nairobi from a provincial political rally such as I witnessed at Eldama Ravine. Mboya's student airlift has become a minor issue in the American Presidential campaign.

The Congo has stumbled from one crisis to another, reminding the world how important and explosive Africa is.

This is modern Africa, a rapidly changing land where men and situations alter before anything written about them can possibly get into print. Yet I came away with several fundamental impressions about Africa that I believe will stand the test of time.

1. The effect of Communism as an ideology in Africa is almost nil; the impact of the Communists as people—the Russians and the Chinese—is tremendous.

2. The Communists have abandoned all overt efforts to win fledgling African states over to Communism. For the moment, the Communists are satisfied if the Africans move out of the Western orbit and accept neutralism. The Communists, I am convinced, believe Africa will drift toward socialism and Communism once it breaks away from the West.

3. Nasser's anti-Zionism doesn't make much sense or impact in black Africa; his concept of a black brotherhood does exert influence. Nasser's good, not his evil, will live after

him. I found Africans leery of Nasser's preoccupation with the Jews but appreciative of his efforts toward removing colonialism and white domination from the continent.

4. For the next five years or so, most of the hot battles in the cold war will be fought in Africa. The Africans will see to that. The Africans have not only learned the art of financing their embryonic states by playing East against West, but they have also learned that every internal conflict can be made a cause for world action if the East-West conflict is interjected. As the Congo demonstrates, both East and West have hidden interests in these African states: these interests come to the fore in terms of an internal conflict that immediately bursts into an international issue.

5. The world is making a grave, if not fatal, mistake by not taking African threats to clear that continent of colonialism and white domination seriously. I am convinced that the Africans mean just what they say and that they will use force only if necessary but fully *expect* that force will be needed.

I am fully confident that the fate of civilization as we know it will be determined in South Africa. If conditions there remain as they are, then I see no alternative to a bloody race war that will in some measure affect every nation in which both white and nonwhite people live. South Africa is like a man with the bubonic plague—everybody in the community could die from his internal problem. This is not a simple problem. Only imaginative, sensitive and farsighted world statesmanship can head off total human disgrace, if not annihilation, in South Africa.

Turning to the shape of things in African states, I find myself racked with mixed emotions.

As an American Negro who is committed to integration, I

am disturbed by African politicians who say white people must get out of politics. It sounds good, and at first hearing it sounds right. The shattering moment comes when one realizes that the Africans are saying that the ethnic majority should form the government in its own image. This argument becomes even more egregious, at least so it seems to me, when the Africans contend that an indigenous people have a right to form the government. This means, for example, that Europeans who have been in South Africa longer than Negroes have been in America have, at best, only squatters' rights.

This, of course, is turn-about. What one sees in Africa is change, not progress; betterment for the black man, but disappointment for the humanist. And for this reason I find virtue in the fact that Africans don't have enough trained people to run their governments. Practical necessity is integration's last hope in Africa.

As Ghana, Guinea, the United Arab Republic and Ethiopia are already demonstrating, it will be some time before democracy as we know it comes to Africa.

This means, of course, that the major African revolt is yet to come. The masses still evidence what Richard Wright calls a "dependency mentality." In time they will demand the right to grow up, they will insist upon sharing the rights, freedoms and advantages now enjoyed by the leadership class. The extension of the African revolt will provide the world, particularly the West, a second chance to express its convictions about the rights of African individuals. This time the cards could well be stacked in favor of the West: so many of the current African leaders are identified with anti-West neutralism it could well be that their opposition will abandon that view. There are moves in this direction in Ghana, Guinea and Ethiopia even now. These moves could be significant, particularly if they can avoid the pitfall of extreme partisanship.

I did not visit West Africa, where racial tensions reportedly are less explosive, and I do not wish to paint all Africa with the same brush. But West Africa is reinvolved in the question of independence as East Africa seeks to shake off the shackles of colonialism and white domination. The crux of Pan-Africanism is that none of Africa is free until all of Africa is divested of nonblack interests, and I am certain that the leaders of West Africa would not part company with East Africans should the latter follow an antiwhite path. Africa—all of it—is a problem for politicians, not writers. Even so, I venture two comments:

First, we would do well to take an all-out stand against racism. The attacks upon whites in the Congo were shocking proof that black men are learning to hate. As a black man, I have seen and felt this hate; it is more than prejudice, it is a desire to destroy.

It occurs to me that private American foundations would do their country and the world a great service if they would underwrite a World Conference on Race Relations—a gathering of various spokesmen in the field of race relations, to arrive at a code of racial fair play. Such a policy could then be urged upon the nations of the world through the United Nations. I have great faith in this suggestion. I feel certain Africans would welcome it as an opportunity to draw world attention to the unbelievable conditions now existing in Mozambique, Angola and Southwest Africa. African settlers would also favor such a conference for it would create an international atmosphere which would protect their civil rights in Africa. From an American point of view, such a conference would give us the initiative, perhaps the leadership, in a broad move to remove racism from the arena of world politics.

Secondly, the United Nations has a natural role in Africa. But it must find a way to join issues *before,* not after, they explode in violence and the world powers have chosen sides. The case of Southwest Africa, it seems to me, affords an excellent opportunity for preventative action. Practically every student of Africa holds that South Africa has illegally annexed Southwest Africa. In his recent book, *The Death of Africa,* Peter Ritner flatly suggests that a United Nations army march into Southwest Africa under the same legal sponsorship that put Tanganyika, also a former League of Nations trust, under the United Nations. I agree, but I feel South Africa would yield if she knew the remainder of the world really meant business.

Modern Africa is an unmistakable call for the return to basic human principles. The big powers cannot on the one hand spout liberal sentiments about freedom and civil rights while supplying arms to South Africa and Portugal with the other. This is particularly true since the same big powers that do business with these oppressive nations have called for a ban on the sale of arms to Africans. This is not an easy matter to resolve. It goes to the heart of the Western defense machine. But what will it profit the West if it gains a maximum of external security and then dies from the internal cancer of racism?

For racism is the irritant on Africa's raw nerves—not colonialism, but that *white* people have colonized *black* people;

not settler domination, but that *white* settlers have dominated indigenous *black* people; not economic exploitation, but that *white* people have exploited *black* people; not social discrimination, but that the *white* power structure sets itself apart from *black* masses; not denial of civil rights, but that *white* people deny *black* people their civil rights.

Africa is pained by change but the absence of good will makes the pain acute. As Africa pains the world hurts with her and for the same reasons.

Through the United Nations, then, the world states must put their economic and political power behind individual freedom and national sovereignty for all peoples. As civilized states they can no longer afford to do less; as practical and sensible human beings, my African brothers dare not ask for more.

ABOUT THE AUTHOR

Louis E. Lomax was born in Valdosta, Georgia, on August 16, 1922. His mother, Sarah, died shortly after he was born and Lomax fell under the guardianship of his maternal grandmother, Rozena Lomax, a well-known writer of religious plays. In the mid-thirties, when he was a high school teenager, Lomax received his first by-line—in the Valdosta *Daily Times*. The *Times* held a contributors' contest which asked readers to submit interesting stories about south Georgia history. Lomax won honorable mention with his story about the night Valdosta was panicked by pranksters who doused a vulture in gasoline, set it on fire and freed it to fly over the town.

After finishing Dasher High School, Lomax attended Paine College in Augusta, Georgia, and became editor of the college paper, *The Paineite*. His career as a professional writer began with the *Afro-American*.

After doing graduate work at American University, Lomax joined the faculty of Georgia State College, in Savannah, where he served as assistant professor of philosophy. Subsequently he did additional graduate study at Yale University, and became a staff feature writer for the Chicago *American*. His articles have also appeared in *Harper's, Life, Pageant, The Nation* and *The New Leader*. In 1959 Lomax joined Mike Wallace's news staff in New York and became the first member of his race to appear on television as a newsman. He and his wife live in Jamaica, New York.

Set in Linotype Caledonia
Format by Jean Krulis
Manufactured by The Haddon Craftsmen, Inc.
Published by HARPER & BROTHERS, *New York*